Concept Maps and CogLab Online Manual

for

Goldstein's

Cognitive Psychology:
Connecting Mind, Research,
and Everyday Experience

Concept Maps and CogLab Online Manual
for
Goldstein's

Cognitive Psychology: Connecting Mind, Research, and Everyday Experience

Concept Maps by
E. Bruce Goldstein
University of Pittsburgh

Concept Maps designed by
Randall Baker

CogLab material created by
Angie MacKewn
University of Tennessee at Martin

With CogLab contributions from
Greg Francis, Ian Neath, and Danalee Goldthwaithe

THOMSON
WADSWORTH

Australia • Canada • Mexico • Singapore • Spain • United Kingdom • United States

Printed in the United States of America
1   2   3   4   5   6   7   07 06 05 04

Printer: Darby Printing

0-534-57727-X

For more information about our products, contact us at:
Thomson Learning Academic Resource Center
1-800-423-0563

For permission to use material from this text or product, submit a request online at
http://www.thomsonrights.com
Any additional questions about permissions can be submitted at
thomsonrights@thomson.com

Thomson Wadsworth
10 Davis Drive
Belmont, CA 94002-3098
USA

Asia
Thomson Learning
5 Shenton Way #01-01
UIC Building
Singapore 068808

Australia/New Zealand
Thomson Learning
102 Dodds Street
Southbank, Victoria 3006
Australia

Canada
Nelson
1120 Birchmount Road
Toronto, Ontario M1K 5G4
Canada

Europe/Middle East/South Africa
Thomson Learning
High Holborn House
50/51 Bedford Row
London WC1R 4LR
United Kingdom

Latin America
Thomson Learning
Seneca, 53
Colonia Polanco
11560 Mexico D.F.
Mexico

Spain/Portugal
Paraninfo
Calle/Magallanes, 25
28015 Madrid, Spain

Table of Contents

CONCEPT MAPS

These concept maps are designed to help you organize and remember the basic concepts presented in this book. These maps, and the questions associated with them, plus the *Test Yourself* questions in each chapter, will help you (1) focus on the key concepts in the book and (2) cite the evidence psychologists have obtained to support these concepts.

How the Concept Maps are Organized

To understand how the maps are organized, look at Map 1.1 on page 1. You can see that this map is organized into three levels. Level 1, indicated by the circle on the left, is the **central-concept level**. This concept is often similar to a major heading in the chapter. Level 2, indicated by the rectangles directly above and below the circle, is the **secondary-concept level**. Level 3, indicated by the rectangles on the right, is the **evidence level.** This evidence is most often experiments or examples from everyday experience that are described in the book (indicated by **E**). In addition, three other types of information are included at this level: methods used to collect data (**M**), basic principles (**P**), and examples that you can supply from your own experiences (**Y**). There is no "Y" box in this particular map, but there are some Y-boxes in later chapters. For example, Map 4.3 asks you to think of an example from your experience in which practice enabled you to improve your ability to divide your attention between two different tasks.

These maps have a top-to-bottom organization. The secondary-concept that appears first in the book is positioned above the circle and is labeled "A". The one that appears next is positioned below the circle and is labeled "B". Some maps have an additional secondary-level concept, which is labeled "C." The "evidence," on the right, is also organized so reading from the top down you will encounter each item in the order in which it appears in the book.

How to Use the Concept Maps

The concept maps can be used in a number of ways. Just looking at the overall layout provides an overview of how a section of the book is organized. You might therefore find it helpful to refer to the concept maps as you are reading the book. In addition to providing an overview of a section of the book, the boxes at the evidence level indicate the rationale and supporting evidence for the various concepts.

The evidence level is the key to understanding and remembering the material in your textbook. You can see why this is so by noticing, as you read the text, that every time a concept is introduced, it is followed by the evidence that supports and explains it. Thus, knowing the definition of a concept is just the first step to really understanding it. The next step is to understand the evidence that supports the concept. To help you achieve this, there are questions below each map that expand on what's inside the boxes and which also provide page references to where you can find the answer in your text. Questions about experiments also include the names of the experimenters. You can answer these questions, or take brief notes on them, in the spaces provided next to the boxes.

If you are able to describe the experimental evidence for a concept, or the methods or principles associated with it, you will have a deeper understanding of the concept, and will be more likely to remember it later. The reason for occasionally asking you to think of personal experiences is that relating material to your own experience makes it more meaningful, and also because memory research has shown that generating information that is linked both to yourself and to something you want to remember is an extremely powerful memory aid. Thus, generating some of your own "evidence" will not only make a concept more "real," but will also help you remember it.

In using these concept maps to help you study, it is important to realize that they do not always cover all of the material in a chapter. To be sure you haven't left anything out, refer to the *Test Yourself* questions that appear in your text. These questions not only cover most of the material in the chapter, but provide another way to check your understanding. One study tactic that you might want to try is to first learn the material in the concept maps, and then check your knowledge, and fill in any missing information, by answering the *Test Yourself* questions.

Introduction to CogLab

Welcome to the Cognitive Psychology Online Laboratory (CogLab), a set of Web-based demonstrations of classic experiments and concepts from cognitive psychology. CogLab allows your students to experience a variety of important experimental studies. This experience will help them understand each experiment, the data, and the significance of the study.

CogLab can be accessed anywhere in the world through the Internet with a Web browser that adequately supports the Java programming language. For Microsoft Windows, appropriate web browsers include Netscape 4.7, Internet Explorer 5.0, and Opera 5.11. For Mac OS 8.5-9.2, appropriate web browsers include Internet Explorer 5.0. For Mac OS X appropriate web browsers include OmniWeb 4.0 and Internet Explorer 5.1. Newer versions of all of these web browsers will also work, but older versions are known to have some incompatibilities with CogLab and are not recommended. Other web browsers and operating systems may also work.

CogLab Demonstrations include:

Attention	**Perception**	**Neurocognition**
Attentional Blink	Apparent Motion	Brain Asymmetry
Simon Effect	Müller-Lyer Illusion	Mapping the Blind Spot
Spatial Cueing	Signal Detection	Receptive Fields
Stroop Effect	Visual Search	
Sensory Memory	**Short-Term Memory**	**Working Memory**
Metacontrast Masking	Brown-Peterson	Irrelevant Speech Effect
Modality Effect	Position Error	Memory Span
Partial Report	Sternberg Search	Operation Span
Suffix Effect		Phonological Similarity
Memory Process	**Metamemory**	**Imagery**
Encoding Specificity	False Memory	Link Word
Serial Position	Forgot it All Along	Mental Rotation
Von Restorff Effect	Remember / Know	Mental Scanning
Speech & Language	**Concepts**	**Judgment**
Categorical Perception – Identification	Absolute Identification	Monty Hall
Categorical Perception – Discrimination	Implicit Learning	Risky Decisions
Lexical Decision	Prototypes	Typical Reasoning
Word Superiority		Wason Selection Task

Getting Started with CogLab

CogLab is an Internet-based program that allows you to explore aspects of Cognitive Psychology by participating in various experiments. You use CogLab by pointing your web browser to http://coglab.wadsworth.com.

This section provides you with a quick introduction to getting started with CogLab. For information on individual experiments, you will need to read the instructions for those experiments.

First, you need a Registration code (access code) which is found on a card in the front of the Goldstein Cognitive Psychology: Connecting Mind, Research and Everyday Experience text. You do not need to purchase a separate registration card or access code, everything is on the card found at the front of the Goldstein text. (**If your textbook is used,** you will need to purchase an access code online by going to http://e-catalog.thomsonlearning.com/110/ and entering "CogLab" in the search field. From the found items select the "CogLab E-Pin Code Version" and then follow the ordering instructions. The E-Pin registration number will be given to you immediately after your order is processed.) Your unique registration code (access code) may only be used one-time by you.

Second, go to class to receive your login ID and a password from your instructor.

Third, register your CogLab account over the Internet. If you have any problems following the below instructions, see the Help page on the CogLab site. If the problems are not resolved on the Help page, talk to your instructor or contact the CogLab support staff by email at support@thomsonlearning.com or by calling 1-800-423-0563.

1. Point your web browser to http://coglab.wadsworth.com. Click on the link *Access your account* under the heading *Students* (near the bottom of the page) to access your account.

2. At the bottom of the new page are two fields. Type your login ID in the top field and your password in the bottom field. It will look something like this:

Enter your assigned information	
Enter your ID:	Francis200F02-1
Enter your password:	*******
Access account	Submit Information

In this example, the login ID is Francis200F02-1. The password is in the field below, which displays each key press as an asterisk. Your login ID will be different. It is what was given to you by your instructor.

3. Click on the *Submit Information* button. Your computer will connect with the CogLab computer over the Internet. If the information you entered is correct, you will see a window like the one below that asks you to enter your registration code (access code).

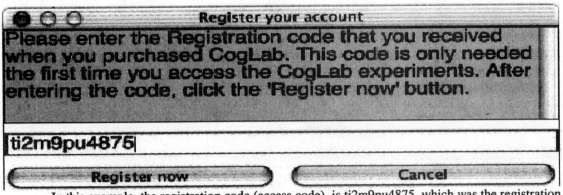

In this example, the registration code (access code) is ti2m9pu4875, which was the registration code (access code) that was printed on a registration card. (Note: You cannot use this particular registration code. Each registration code (access code) works only one time.) If you click on the *Register now* button, your computer will send information over the Internet to the CogLab computer and verify the registration code. If the information is correct, the account will be registered and ready for use. Once a CogLab account is registered, you will not need the registration code again (nor can it be used a second time). For all future interactions with CogLab, you will need only your login ID and password.

4. You will now find that the button labeled *Access account* on the web page is enabled. Clicking on that button will open a new window called "User information".

User information

		Labs you have finished
Group name:	PSY 200, Purdue University	
Your login ID:	Francis200F02-1	
Registration code:	ti2m9pu4875	
Date registered:	Aug 12, 2002 11:44:43 AM	
Identifying name:		
Password (6-10 characters):	************	
Verify the password:	************	
Email:		
Security Question:		
Security Answer:		

Get your data

Get group averages

| Apply | Cancel/Close | **Get group trial–by–trial** |

This is your current account information

In this window enter your name (most instructors want the family name first, first name last; e.g., Smith, John) in the field next to the label *Identifying name*: If you wish, you can also change your password by entering the new password in the two appropriate text fields.

CogLab has a feature (new for Fall 2003) that will send you your password via email if you forget it. This feature will work only if you enter your email address and a question and answer. If you forget your password, the CogLab system will ask you the question that you enter here. If you then enter the answer that you've entered here, CogLab will email you your password. If you choose to use this feature and enter a valid email address, this email address will be used only for sending you your password. You will not receive any other email from or about CogLab, and your email address will not be provided to anybody else. It is up to you whether you enter a valid email address, but if you do not, then this password reminder feature will not work.

5.   Click on the *Apply* button to save the changes. If you click on the *Cancel/Close* button, none of the changes you've made will be saved.

6.   You can return to this web page later and access other features of your CogLb account. For example, once you have completed some labs, they will be listed on the right side of the User information window. You can select a lab and click on one of the buttons to view either your own data, averages of the entire group, or group trial-by-trial data.

Fourth, start running experiments. To run an experiment, click on the link to that experiment from the main CogLab page (http://coglab.wadsworth.com). On the bottom of each page, there will be a place to enter your login ID and password. Do not go to the *Access your account* web page to run demos.

Note: If you never get a response from the CogLab computer and/or web browser hangs after clicking the *Submit password* button, you may be behind a firewall. Have your instructor contact the CogLab support staff (support@thomsonlearning.com or 1-800-423-0563) for information on how to work around the firewall.

Running a CogLab Experiment

STEP 1: RUNNING THE EXPERIMENT

Each experiment's web page has unique instructions that describe details of experimental stimuli and the experimental task. To properly complete a demonstration, you *must* read and understand the instructions. You will not be able to complete an experiment unless you understand the instructions. Click on the *Start experiment* button to begin the experiment. Your computer will connect with the CogLab computer to download the necessary files. This may take a minute or more, depending on the speed of your Internet connection. A window will appear where experimental stimuli will be presented and your responses will be measured. On this experiment window there is a menu option labeled "Instructions." Selecting this menu will open a new window with instructions on what you need to do during the experiments. Most experiments require you to press a key or click on a button to start an experimental trial. You must read the instructions to know what is required to get the experiment running.

STEP 2: FINISHING THE EXPERIMENT

When you finish an experiment, the experiment window will close and your computer will connect to the CogLab computer through the Internet and automatically store your data. After a short delay, a summary of your data will appear. *Wait for this window to appear before closing your web browser.* The first line of the summary window will confirm that your data has been saved. The data is available for both you and your instructor to download later. If Internet usage is heavy, it may take a few minutes for the window to appear. The windows below demonstrate what is seen (on Windows 98) after completing the Mental rotation experiment.

Your data has been saved on the CogLab server. You can check your CogLab account by going to the Student Access page.

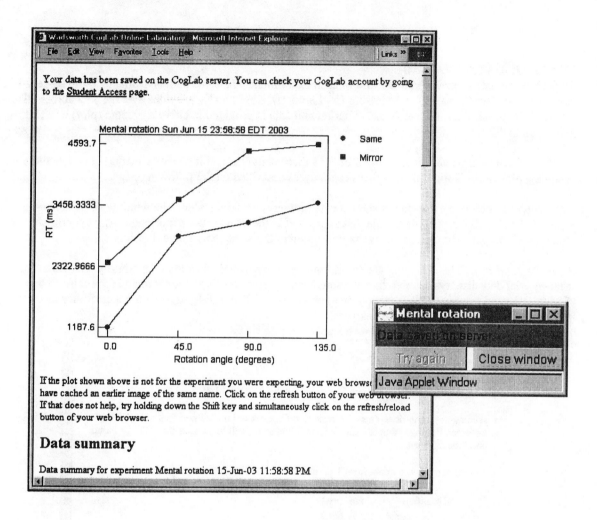

If the plot shown above is not for the experiment you were expecting, your web browse have cached an earlier image of the same name. Click on the refresh button of your web browser. If that does not help, try holding down the Shift key and simultaneously click on the refresh/reload button of your web browser.

Data summary

Data summary for experiment Mental rotation 15-Jun-03 11:58:58 PM

Working with CogLab Data

TYPES OF DATA AVAILABLE

Experimental data is produced at the end of each experiment. The same data is available to the student and instructor (see the steps for Accessing CogLab data). CogLab also provides average data across all the students in the class. In every case, experimental data is provided in either a graphic (plot) or a text (table) format.

Data plot: This is a graphical description of the experimental data. Not all experiments show data plots. The data plot can be imported into other programs, as described on the following pages.

Data table: Experiments that do not show a data plot, present a data table. The window below shows an example (on MacOS X) of a data table that appears after the Stroop task experiment. Any experiment that contains a data plot also includes a data table version of the same experimental results.

Trial-by-Trial data: The data generated at the end of an experiment also includes trial-by-trial data. The trial-by-trial data displays detailed information about the stimulus (e.g., the word and font color in the Stroop task) and response (e.g., reaction time) on each trial. The trial-by-trial data are useful for performing some types of statistical analyses.

Wadsworth CogLab Online Laboratory

Data summary

Data summary for experiment Stroop task Feb 12, 2003 11:39:35 AM

Average reaction times (ms) for same or different word names and font colors. The expected finding is that RT for name and font same will be smaller than RT for name and font different.

Results are based on data from 1 participants.

Condition	RT (ms)
Name and font same:	569.6667
Name and font different:	692.7

Trial by trial data

Stroop task trial by trial data. Feb 12, 2003 11:39:35 AM Data presented in order of presentation. Note that precision of RT varies across computers.

Trial	User ID	Word	Font color	RT (ms)
0	Francis200F02-1	GREEN	green	875.0
1	Francis200F02-1	GREEN	blue	1032.0
2	Francis200F02-1	RED	green	843.0
3	Francis200F02-1	BLUE	green	734.0
4	Francis200F02-1	RED	green	750.0

You may wish to integrate CogLab experimental data into your class lecture or to apply a statistical analysis. Working with CogLab data requires that you transfer the data to your personal computer.

PRINTING OR SAVING DATA

The experimental data produced at the end of an experiment are presented in a new window in the web browser. Use the printing and/or saving functions of your web browser to print or save the data.

IMPORTING DATA INTO A SPREADSHEET

The data tables presented by CogLab follow the standard conventions for creating tables on web pages. When you select, copy, and paste the data into a spreadsheet, the separate cells of the data table will automatically be placed in appropriate cells of the spreadsheet. This allows easy portability of CogLab data into programs that use spreadsheets, such as *MS Excel*, *SPSS*, *SigmaPlot*, and many others (as can be seen in the graphic below). If you save the experimental data to a file on your computer, you can open the file with a variety of programs that can read web pages (e.g., *MS Word* and *MS Excel*). This will also import a data plot into the program. This is useful for students preparing reports.

Microsoft Excel - Book2

File Edit View Insert Format Tools Data Window Help

Arial

C10 = Same

	A	B	C	D	E	F
1	Trial	User ID	Stimuli	Rotation	RT (ms)	
2	0	user0	Same	0	830	
3	1	user0	Same	45	1160	
4	2	user0	Same	0	830	
5	3	user0	Same	45	980	
6	4	user0	Same	90	880	
7	5	user0	Mirror	135	1760	
8	6	user0	Mirror	0	990	
9	7	user0	Mirror	45	1370	
10	8	user0	Same	90	2250	
11	9	user0	Same	135	1260	
12	10	user0	Same	90	2310	
13	11	user0	Same	45	720	
14	12	user0	Same	135	1370	
15	13	user0	Same	0	820	
16	14	user0	Same	45	930	

Sheet1 / Sheet2 / Sheet3 /

CogLab FAQ

Why do the CogLab windows say "Warning: Java Applet window", or something similar?
The CogLab programs are written in the Java programming language, which is run within your web browser. There is potentially much danger in running programs on the Internet because a malicious program could delete files or copy personal information. As a security feature, web browsers make every Java window have a statement that explicitly describes it as a Java window. The message varies across web browsers. You do not need to be worried about the Java window or do anything about the warning message.

Sometimes CogLab does not seem to respond to my requests. What is going on?
Most likely there is Internet congestion between your computer and CogLab. If the Internet is very busy, it may take over a minute before CogLab responds to your request. The actual time required will depend on Internet congestion, use of CogLab, your physical distance from the CogLab computer, and the amount of information being sent.

Why do I get the "access denied" message?
You are probably entering some of your account information incorrectly. This information is case sensitive. For example, "user52" is not the same as "User52". Your instructor can verify that you have the correct account information and password.

Why doesn't the experiment begin?
If a window appears to start the experiment but nothing seems to happen, make certain that you are following the directions. Most experiments require you to press a key or click on a button to start an experimental trial. If the instructions ask you to press a key to start a trial, but nothing happens after the key press, your web browser may be causing a minor problem. Some web browsers fail to properly direct keyboard input to the designated window. Using your mouse, click once in the middle of the window. (Be sure to move the mouse cursor out of the way of any stimuli that may be presented). Pressing the appropriate key should now produce a response from the window.

Why aren't some of the experiments working on my Linux system?
There is a known problem with many X window managers such that text is not drawn to the screen unless some other activity (e.g., moving the mouse) occurs. This affects demos such as Attentional Blink and Lexical Decision. Try a different window manager/web browser combination.

Why don't I see a data summary or graph at the end of the experiment?
If your web browser freezes at the end of the experiment, you may have lost your Internet connection. Many operating systems (including Windows 95/98) automatically hang up the modem connection after a period of inactivity. You can adjust this; details should be available from the help menu of your operating system.

If your modem is still connected to the Internet there may be a lot of Internet traffic at this time. At the end of every experiment your computer connects with the CogLab server to send information back and forth. You may need to wait a few minutes.

How do I print the data summary or graph?
When the data loads in a web browser window, use the printing capabilitied of your web browser (usually in the "File" menu).

Why won't CogLab let me register?
To register on CogLab, you will need a unique registration code. This is printed on the inside of your copy of the CogLab Student Manual or on the bottom of the registration card. In addition to this registration code, your instructor should provide you with a groupID, a userID, and a password. Make sure you enter the information exactly as written. If you are still experiencing difficulties, please contact Tech Support at: email: support@kdc.com or phone: 800-423-0563

Why did I get a "Security Error" message?
This message is mostly likely the result of a security program that has been installed on your computer. This type of program can prevent the CogLab program from sending data back to the CogLab server. Out of concern for security on the Internet, some universities (or individuals) install various programs to prevent malicious programs from snooping on your computer. CogLab programs do not read any information from your hard drive. However, if the settings in these security programs are set very high, the act of communicating to another computer may set them off. If these security programs prevent you from finishing an assigned experiment, then you will have to change the security settings (or ask the computer lab manager to do so), or use a computer without this security program.

Why doesn't the "Trials to Go" menu count down?
If the Trials to go menu is not counting down it may be for one of two reasons. First, some very old web browsers seem to have a bug that prevents changes to a menu label. As a result, the experiment is counting down the trials, but the menu does not show it. If this is the case, the experiment will end when you complete all the trials.

Second, some experiments require that you provide a correct answer(s) on each trial. When mistakes occur, the trial is repeated later in the experiment. If you never answer correctly, the Trials to go menu label properly shows that you have not completed any trials. Until you provide the correct answers for the trials the experiment will not end. Make sure you read the instructions for that experiment.

Why doesn't the window fill the entire screen?
Some experiments create a window that fills the entire screen, but not all of them do. The instructions indicate when that is to be expected. However, some very old browsers do not properly implement some parts of Java, and as a result, windows that should be full screen are not. If you are supposed to get a full-screen window but do not and you are using a very old browser, try switching to a more recent version.

What web browsers work best?
Microsoft Windows XP
Microsoft included Java with some version of Windows XP but did not include it with other versions. Even if Java was included, some of the earlier versions of Windows XP included a version of Java that does not work well with some of the demos (e.g., Muller-Lyer). You can fix this problem by installing Microsoft's Service Pack 1.

Although most of the demos work properly with Netscape 6.2, some of them (especially those in which presentation of stimuli is very brief) do not work properly.

All other versions of Microsoft Windows (e.g., 95, 98, etc.)
Use one of the following:
Internet Explorer 5.0
Mozilla 1.0
Netscape 4.7
Opera 5.11

Apple MacOS X
Make sure you are **not** using JVM version 1.4.1 (released on March 10, 2003). Rather, keep using JVM version 1.3.1 and use one of the following:
Internet Explorer 5.2
OmniWeb 4.1

Apple Mac OS 8.5-9.2
Make sure you have the most recent version of Apple's implementation of Java, MRJ (available from Apple at http://developer.apple.com/java/download.html). Please note: Neither Netscape Navigator nor Netscape Communicator with version numbers of 3.x or 4.x will work. Instead, use:
Internet Explorer 5.1.6

Newer versions of all of these web browsers will also work, but older versions are known to have incompatibilities with CogLab.

How do I contact Tech Support?
If your question is not answered below, please contact our Tech Support. The best way is to use the web-based form, as it prompts you for the information necessary for Tech Support to help you quickly. However, email and phone support is also available.
1. Web: http://coglab.wadsworth.com/support/techsupport.html
2. Email: support@thomsonlearning.com
3. Phone 800-423-0563

1.1 HISTORY I

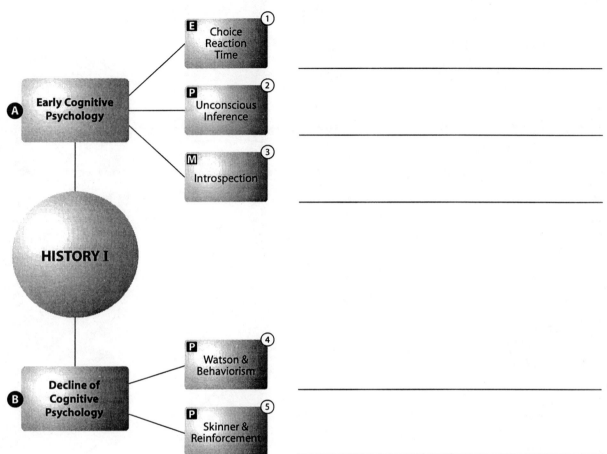

A Why can we say that cognitive psychology began in the 19th Century, even though there was no field called "cognitive psychology" at the time?

① **Experiment:** What was the rationale behind Donders' RT experiment? Be able to relate this experiment to Figure 1.4. (Donders; 6)

② **Principle:** What is the principle of unconscious inference? Why was it proposed? (Helmholtz; 7)

③ **Method:** Describe the method of analytic introspection and give an example of a situation in which it might be used. (8)

B Why did most psychologists lose interest in studying the mind, beginning early in the 1900's?

④ **Principle:** What principle of behaviorism led psychologists to reject the study of the mind? (Watson; 9)

⑤ **Principle:** What was the main focus of Skinner's research and how did it reflect the goals of behaviorism? (Skinner; 10)

1.2 HISTORY II

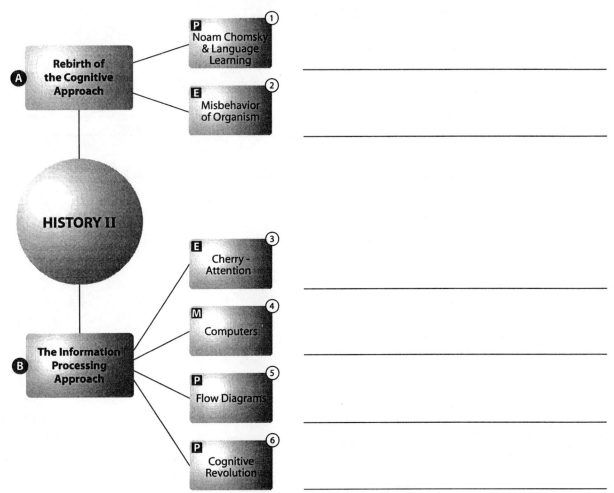

A What events began occurring in the 1950's and 1960's, which led to the "rebirth" of the study of the mind?

① **Principle:** What were Chomsky's criticisms of Skinner's book *Verbal Behavior*? (10)

② **Experiment:** What conclusion was drawn from a raccoon's "misbehavior" in an operant conditioning experiment? (Breland & Breland; 11)

B What is the idea behind the information processing approach?

③ **Experiment:** Describe Cherry's attention experiment. Why was it important? (Cherry; 12)

④ **Method:** Describe two ways that the first computers were used to study the mind. (13)

⑤ **Principle:** What inspired the development of flow diagrams that were designed to represent what is happening in the mind? (13)

⑥ **Principles:** When was the "birthday" of cognitive psychology? Was there a "cognitive revolution"? (14)

1.3 A MODERN COGNITIVE PSYCHOLOGY EXPERIMENT

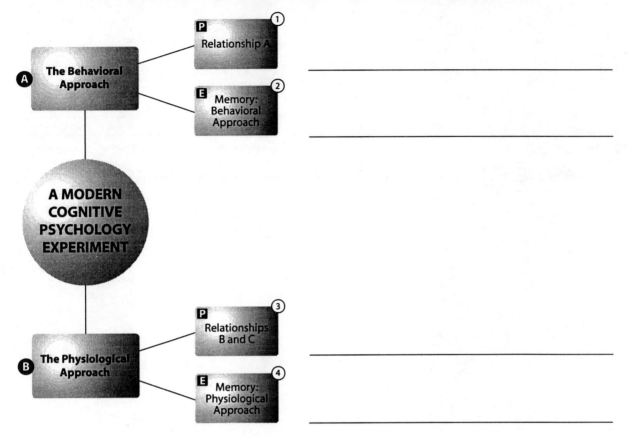

A **What is the behavioral approach to the study of the mind?**

① **Principle:** Which relationship in the flow diagram of Figure 1.9 is measured when taking a behavioral approach to the study of the mind? How can this be applied to Donders' RT experiment? (15)

② **Experiment:** Describe the behavioral part of Davachi's memory experiment. Be sure you understand the connection between what she measured and one of the relationships in Figure 1.9. (Davachi; 16)

B **What is the physiological approach to the study of the mind?**

③ **Principle:** Which relationships in the flow diagram of Figure 1.9 are measured when taking a physiological approach to the study of the mind? How could this be applied to a modern version of Donders' RT experiment? (15)

④ **Experiment:** Describe the physiological part of Davachi's memory experiment. Be sure you understand the connection between what she measured and the relationships in Figure 1.9. (Davachi; 18)

Stroop Effect

When you first learned to tie shoelaces you needed to carefully think through each step of the process. Now, you probably do not even seem to think about the steps, but simply initiate a series of movements that seem to proceed without any further influence. When a behavior or skill seems to no longer require direct interaction, cognitive psychologists say it is automatized.

Many behaviors can become automatized: typing, reading, writing, bicycling, piano playing, driving, etc. Automatization is interesting because it is an important part of daily life. We perform a variety of automatized behaviors quickly and effortlessly. In some cases people report that they do not consciously know how the behavior is performed, they just will it to happen, and it does happen.

To explore properties of automatized behaviors cognitive psychologists often put observers in a situation where an automatized response is in conflict with the desired behavior. This allows researchers to test the behind-the-scenes properties of automatized behaviors by noting their influence on more easily measured behaviors. This demonstration explores a well-known example of this type of influence, the Stroop effect.

Stroop (1935) noted that observers were slower to properly identify the color of ink when the ink was used to produce color names different from the ink. That is, observers were slower to identify red ink when it spelled the word blue. This is an interesting finding because observers are told to not pay any attention to the word names and simply report the color of the ink. However, this seems to be a nearly impossible task, as the name of the word seems to interfere with the observer's ability to report the color of the ink.

A common explanation for the Stroop effect is that observers (especially college undergraduates) have automatized the process of reading. Thus, the color names of the words are always processed very quickly, regardless of the color of the ink. On the other hand, identifying colors is not a task that observers have to report on very often, and because it is not automatized it is slower. The fast and automatic processing of the color name of the word interferes with the reporting of the ink color.

The Stroop task, and its many variations, is a commonly used tool in cognitive psychology to explore how different types of behaviors interact. This demonstration allows you to participate in a simple version of the Stroop task.

For registration information go to http://coglab.wadsworth.com.

After clicking on the start the button, a window will appear to start the experiment. Start a trial by pressing the space bar. A fixation dot will appear in the middle of the window, stare at it. A short time later (less than a second) a word (RED, GREEN, or BLUE) will appear on the screen, and the word will be drawn in red, green, or blue font color. Your task is to classify, as quickly as possible, the font color, regardless of the word name. If the font color is red, press the h key; for green, press the j key; for blue, press the k key. It may take a bit of practice to make certain you remember which key corresponds to which font color.

After pressing a key to identify the font color, you will receive feedback on whether you were correct. If you were incorrect the trial will be repeated later in the experiment. If you find you are making lots of mistakes you should slow down, or make certain you understood which key goes with which font color. Press the space bar to start the next trial. If you wish, before pressing the space bar, but after identifying the font color, you can check how many trials remain for the current experiment with the pull-down menu.

There are at least 45 trials, 30 where the font colors and word names are different and 15 where the font colors and color names match (e.g., the word RED in red font color). You can also discard a trial by pressing the t key instead of identifying the font color. Discarding is appropriate if, after starting a trial, you sneeze, zone out, or are otherwise distracted. Discarded trials will be repeated later.

At the end of the experiment a new window will appear that reports the reaction time in milliseconds for identifying the font color when the word names and colors match and when they are different. You should find that the reaction time is longer when the word names and colors are different.

Additional References

Cohen, J. D., Dunbar, K. & McClelland, J. L. (1990). On the control of automatic processes: A parallel distributed processing account of the Stroop effect. *Psychological Review, 97* (3), 332-361.

Cox, C. S., Chee, E., Chase, G. A., Baumgardner, T. L., Schuerholz, L. J., & Reader, M. J. (1997). Reading proficiency affects the construct validity of the Stroop test interference score. *Clinical Neuropsychologist, 11*, 105-110.

Davidson, D. J, Zacks, R. J., & Williams, C. C. (2003). Stroop interference, practice, and aging. *Aging Neuropsychology and Cognition, 10*, (2) 85-98.

MacLeod, C. M. (1991). Half a century of research on the Stroop effect: An integrative review. *Psychological Bulletin, 109*, 163-203.

MacLeod, C. M., & Bors, D. A. (2002). Presenting two color words on a single Stroop trial: Evidence for joint influence, not capture. *Memory & Cognition, 30*, 789-797.

Basic Questions

1. What was the independent variable in this experiment? What are the levels of the independent measure? What was the dependent variable? How was the dependent variable measured?

2. In this experiment, if you made an error, that trial was repeated later. How could you change the dependent measure in this experiment so that this did not occur?

3. Jim works in a glass recycling plant and is responsible for sorting the colored glass into the different bins for processing. Jim is thankful for this job because he only has a grade 9 education. How do you think Jim would do on the Stroop test? Explain your answer.

4. Do you think that practice would decrease the Stroop effect?

5. Do you think that the Stroop effect would be present in individuals who weren't fluent readers? Why or why not?

Advanced Questions

1. How could the Stroop test be used in clinical psychology to identify phobias, for example if Joe is afraid of spiders?

2. What would you expect the results of a Stroop test to be for a bilingual person? Do you think that the Stroop effect would be equal for both languages? Explain your answer.

3. Explain how automatization is related to the Stroop effect. Use the variables of this lab to help explain your answer.

Discussion Questions

1. You can see how the Stroop test is used in clinical psychology, as shown in the above question. In what other ways could the Stroop test be used as pre-and post-tests or as general tests of cognitive ability or alertness in clinical and applied psychology?

2. How do you think older adults perform on the Stroop test compared to younger adults? Explain your answer in terms of cognitive processing.

2.1 PHYSIOLOGICAL: SIGNALS & COMMUNICATION

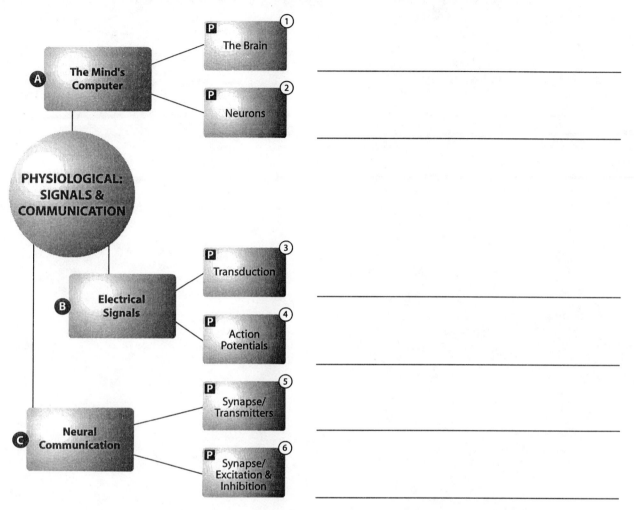

A   Why is it accurate to call the brain a computer?

①   **Principle:** Describe the basic layout of the brain by indicating its main structures and their functions. (26)

②   **Principle:** Describe the neuron and its structure. (28)

B   How is electricity created and transmitted in the nervous system?

③   **Principle:** What is transduction? Give examples of transduction in a mechanical device and in the nervous system. (30)

④   **Principle:** What happens to the charge inside an axon during an action potential? How does the firing of action potentials change when the intensity of the stimulus is increased? What does it mean to say action potentials are propagated? (31)

C   How does communication occur in the nervous system?

⑤   **Principle:** What is a synapse? How do neural signals get across the synapse? (33)

⑥   **Principle:** What happens when excitatory or inhibitory neurotransmitters are released at the synapse? (34)

2.2 PHYSIOLOGICAL: PROCESSING, ORGANIZATION & CODING

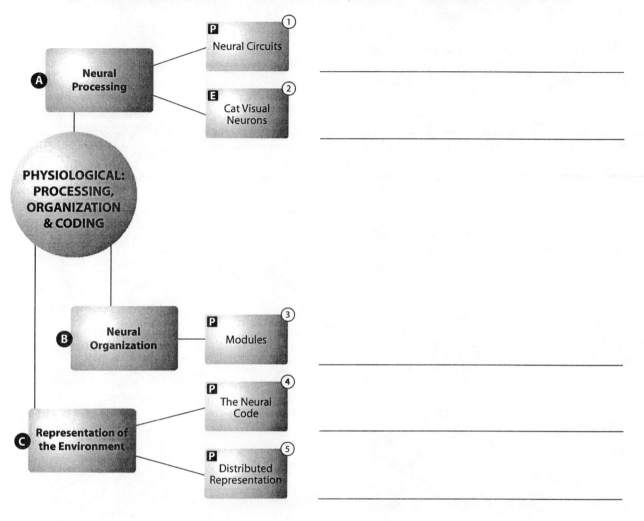

A What does it mean to say that neurons "process information"?

① **Principle:** What is a neural circuit? Be sure you understand how the circuit in Figure 2.13 works. (36)

② **Experiment:** What kinds of visual stimuli cause neurons in the cat's retina and visual cortex to respond? (Hubel & Wiesel; 37)

B How are neurons in the brain organized, based on their function?

③ **Principle:** What is a module? Why have the inferotemporal cortex (IT) and medial temporal cortex (MT) been called modules? (40)

C How are stimuli in the environment represented in the nervous system?

④ **Principle:** What is the "neural code"? What are two ways that a face can be represented by neural responding? Which one of these two possibilities is most likely to be correct? (42)

⑤ **Principle:** What is "distributed activation of the brain"? How can this idea be applied to memory? (44)

2.3 PHYSIOLOGICAL METHODS

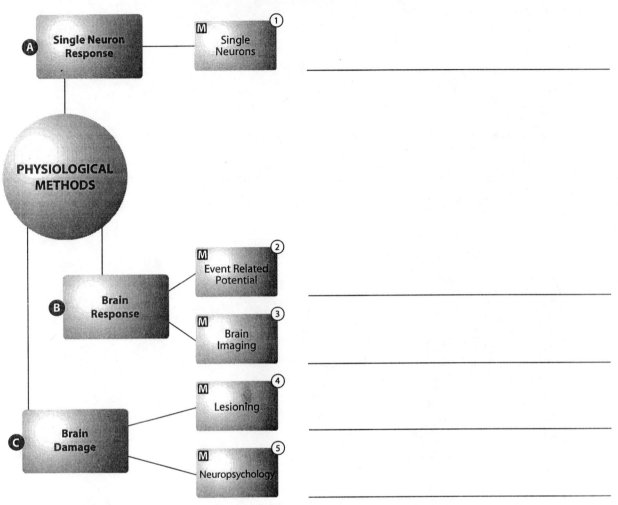

A **What is single unit recording?**

① **Method:** How is single unit activity recorded and what kind of information does it provide? (44)

B **How does the brain respond to stimuli in the environment?**

② **Method:** What is the event related potential (ERP)? How is it recorded and what can it tell us about the functioning of the brain? (47)

③ **Method:** What is the basic principle behind brain imaging? Be able to describe PET, fMRI and the subtraction technique. (48)

C **What can studying the effects of brain damage tell us about the operation of the brain?**

④ **Method:** What is brain lesioning? Describe the case of H. M. (50)

⑤ **Method:** What is neuropsychology? What are dissociations and what do single and double dissociations tell us about how brain functions? (51)

Receptive Fields

A fundamental tenet of cognitive science is that the mind can be understood by studying the brain. The brain consists of billions of individual cells (neurons), whose combined behavior corresponds to what we call cognition. Because of the immense number of neurons and their complicated connections, it is difficult to relate the behavior of an individual neuron with human behavior (e.g., seeing a red apple).

A concept that helps make that connection, in certain cases, is the receptive field. Basically, the receptive field of a neuron consists of any stimulus that changes the neuron's firing rate. By definition, every neuron has a receptive field, although the receptive fields for some neurons are very complicated. The concept of a receptive field is most useful in those parts of the brain that are tied to specific senses (e.g., touch, audition, vision, taste) or to motor control. For neurons sensitive to visual information, for example, the receptive field describes how spatial patterns of light influence the neuron's behavior. It is often the case that a neuron responds only when light falls within a certain part of the visual field. Moreover, the light can have excitatory or inhibitory effects, depending on where it falls in the receptive field. Identifying the region of the receptive field and the excitatory and inhibitory parts provides a good deal of information about the role of the neuron in visual perception.

In a neurophysiological study of visual receptive fields (and there are many), a researcher typically inserts an electrode into a neuron to record its electrical potential (including action potentials). The researcher then presents visual stimuli to the animal and records the cellular responses. By noting changes in the electrical potential (or in the number of action potentials), the researcher can determine if light at a particular location is: (a) excitatory, (b) inhibitory, or (c) outside the receptive field and thus neither excitatory nor inhibitory. By carefully watching the cell's behavior as the stimulus changes, the researcher can map out the receptive field of a neuron.

Knowledge about neural receptive fields is of great significance for understanding perception. For example, neurons close to the retinas of your eyes have (relatively) circularly shaped receptive fields. For some neurons the center of this circle is excitatory, while the surround is inhibitory. Other neurons switch the locations of excitation and inhibition. Some neurons in area V1 of the cortex are sensitive to light-to-dark edges of a specific orientation. Other neurons in area V1 are sensitive to light-to-dark edges but are also sensitive to dark-to-light edges of the same orientation. The properties of these neurons play a fundamental role in theories of visual perception.

This experiment provides you with the opportunity to map out receptive fields. Your task is to find the receptive field, partly identify its excitatory and inhibitory regions, and categorize the neuron based on its receptive field properties. Do not take the properties of the virtual neurons too literally. The receptive fields are caricatures of true receptive fields; they do not take into account much of the underlying neurophysiology. This caveat aside, this experiment will hopefully introduce you to the concept of receptive fields.

For registration information go to http://coglab.wadsworth.com.

Clicking on the practice or experiment buttons below will initiate the different parts of the experiment. A window will appear with three basic components. On the bottom left is a drawing canvas. Here you draw images that are to be presented to the virtual visual system. On the top left is a plot that shows the response of the cell to the most recently submitted image. On the right are checkboxes and buttons for you to guess the neuron category, start the next trial, change the drawing color, submit an image to the virtual visual system, clear the drawing canvas, and show the actual receptive field of the cell.

Your task is to draw a stimulus that generates a response in the neuron that is at least 50% of its maximal response. Once you have that stimulus you can guess the category and move on to the next trial. When you correctly guess the category you can also click on a button to show the true shape of the receptive field.

The practice version is just like the experiment version, except you can always reveal the true shape of the receptive field by clicking on the Show RF button. It is a good idea to start with the practice version because it allows you to see the receptive field and explore how light patterns correspond to electrical potentials. A shown receptive field is represented on the drawing canvas by a green (excitatory) region and a red (inhibitory) region. The locations of the green and red pixels correspond to the location in visual space of the receptive field. With the mouse, click in the middle of the green region and then click on the Submit image button. You should see that the plot of electrical potential shows a small hill. Each image submission corresponds to presenting the drawn image (not the red and green, only what you draw) to the virtual animal for 300 milliseconds. The electrical potential rises at stimulus onset (time zero) and falls after stimulus offset (time 300 ms). The spikes plotted intermittently correspond to action potentials. Action potential frequency increases as electrical potential increases, but action potentials can also occur without a stimulus.

Try filling in more and more of the green region with white blocks. When you click on the Submit image button you should find that the neuron gives a stronger and stronger response. Now start filling in some of the red region as well. You will find that the electrical potential is smaller and there are fewer action potentials. When you fill in all of the red and the green you should find that the neuron does not respond to the stimulus any differently than it responds to a blank screen.

You can clear the white you have drawn in two ways. One way is to click on the Clear image button. This clears the screen of everything. The second way is to click on the Draw in black button. This changes the drawing color so that it will draw black squares instead of white squares (it is like a small eraser). Clicking on Draw in white button will return the mouse control to drawing in white again.

Keep exploring with different light patterns until you think you have a pretty good idea how to use the controls and how different light patterns change the neuron's behavior. Draw and submit an image that generates a strong response from the neuron. Click on the checkboxes. A message will appear indicating when you are correct in your categorization of the neuron. You can now click on the Next Trial button to interact with another receptive field.

Your goal is to find and identify the receptive field of the neuron selected for the current trial. The receptive field types and their shapes are shown in the figure below. The simple and complex receptive fields have similar shapes, but the complex receptive field is actually, well, more complex than can be drawn. A complex receptive field can respond to light on either side of its receptive field, but it does not respond well to light on both sides of its receptive field. A simple receptive field is sensitive to light on only one, fixed side. For the simple neuron receptive field, the excitatory and inhibitory sides are randomly chosen.

The practice and experiment programs are nearly identical, except that the show receptive field button is always enabled in the practice version. This is to provide you with an opportunity to learn what types of stimuli are needed to drive the different cell types.

The receptive field will be randomly located on the canvas drawing surface. Your task is to find its location and draw an image that will get the neuron to respond strongly. You can then categorize it and move on to the next trial. Each receptive field is presented once, in random order.

This is a rather challenging experiment to finish. Once you are done you should have a pretty good idea of what a receptive field consists of, and the effects of excitation and inhibition. When you finish categorizing the last receptive field, a new window will appear that reports the time it took you to categorize each receptive field. Consider the effort neurophysiologists must exert to explore the receptive fields of real neurons.

Additional References

Olshausen, B. A., & Field, D. J. (1996). Emergence of simple-cell receptive field properties by learning a sparse code for natural images. *Nature, 381*, 607-609.

Mechler, F. & Ringach, D. L. (2002). On the classification of simple and complex cells. *Vision Research, 42*, 1017-1033.

Tailor, D. R., Finkel, L. H., & Buchsbaum, G. (2000). Color-opponent receptive fields derived from independent component analysis of natural images. *Vision Research, 40*, 2671-2676.

Walker, G. A., Ohzawa, I. & Freeman, R. D. (2000). Suppression outside the classical cortical receptive field. *Visual Neuroscience, 17,* 1-11.

Basic Questions

1. What is a receptive field of a neuron?

2. What does the receptive fields of the neurons look like around the retina?

3. How are action potentials related to the visual receptive field?

4. Do you think the visual system is more sensitive to overall light intensity or contrasts in light intensities?

Advanced Questions

1. What is the difference between excitatory and inhibitory receptors?

2. How do you think the firing rate of a neuron with a large receptive field compares to a neuron with a small receptive field?

Discussion Questions

1. Discuss how the receptive field is related to attention.

2. Discuss how an electrode can be used to measure and map out receptive fields.

Brain Asymmetry

You may have heard that each person has two distinct hemispheres of the brain, with different capabilities. For example, the sensory signals from the left side of your body are sent to the right hemisphere of your brain; and the sensory signals from the right side of your body are sent to the left hemisphere of your brain. Likewise, control of your right arm and leg is via your left hemisphere; and control of your left arm and leg is via your right hemisphere. More notable cognitive differences also exist. The left hemisphere is said to deal with language and analytical thought, while the right hemisphere is said to deal with spatial relations and creativity. The basis for these claims about cognition comes from investigations of clinical patients who, usually to control a serious case of epilepsy, underwent a surgery that separated their left and right hemispheres. (This surgery prevented epileptic seizures from passing from one hemisphere to the other.) Careful studies of these split-brain patients revealed fascinating properties about how the brain was organized. A patient asked to fixate on a spot on a screen could verbally report words flashed on the right side of the screen (those words were sent to the left hemisphere). The patient could not say the word if it was flashed on the left side of the screen (thus sent to the right hemisphere). Notably, the patient could identify, by picking up with the left hand a physical item matching a word flashed on the left side of the screen.

Subsequent work showed a variety of differences between the brain hemispheres, and some researchers concluded that even people without split brains effectively have two competing brains. These conclusions were picked up by the popular press, and one now sees a variety of claims that schools should nurture one brain side instead of another, or that different types of therapy should be used to strengthen an undeveloped hemisphere.

Some of these claims appear in very odd places. For example, unrelated research suggests that Mozart's music stimulates creativity and intelligence in children. One CD jacket claims that Mozart's music stimulates the left-brain to improve logical skills. It suggests positioning the speakers on the child's right side (presumably so the sound goes to the left brain). It is nice music and may help improve logical skills, but the left-brain, right-brain difference does not necessarily have anything to do with it. Moreover, sound will go in both ears and reach both hemispheres, so positioning the speakers on one side versus another cannot possibly make much difference.

As it turns out, it is rather difficult to find much difference at all between the two hemispheres in normals (individuals without split-brain surgery). This is not to suggest that there are no differences, but the functional significance of these differences may be very slight. Moreover, when such differences do exist, they tend to be strongest for right-handed males. Females and left-handed individuals tend to not show brain-side effects nearly as well.

This experiment lets you search for differences between your left and right hemispheres. It is an unusual experiment in that it is quite possible that you will not find an effect. Given the pervasive nature of the left-brain, right-brain belief, however, a person knowledgeable about cognitive psychology should recognize how difficult it can be to demonstrate such effects.

Your task is to categorize stimuli as quickly as possible. Stimuli will be words or shapes. The stimuli will appear on either the left side of the display (and thus go to your right hemisphere) or on the right side of the display (and thus go to your left hemisphere). If the left hemisphere is really more strongly involved in language processing, you might expect that words presented on the right side of the screen will be responded to faster than words presented on the left side of the screen. Likewise, shapes presented to the left side of the screen might be responded to faster because they are sent to the right hemisphere, which deals with spatial and geometrical information.

For registration information go to http://coglab.wadsworth.com.

The demonstration is split into two experiments that are run in succession. Start by clicking on the button below. A window will appear. After positioning the mouse in the window, press the space bar. A fixation dot will appear in the middle of the window, stare at it and make a concerted effort to not move your eyes during an experimental trial. One to two seconds later a green shape will appear, either on the right or the left side of the screen. Your task is to determine whether the shape is a circle (press the / key) or a square (press the z key). You will be given feedback on whether your classification was correct. After pressing the z or / key, press the space bar to start the next trial.

There are at least 80 shape classifications to be made, with equal numbers of shapes and sides of presentation. It should not concern you which side of the screen the shape is drawn. Simply note whether the shape is a circle or a square.

After running the shape experiment, the program will immediately start to run an experiment involving the classification of words. The word stimuli are all verbs and your task is to classify each verb as present or past tense. The present tense words are FALL, RUN, SEE, SHOOT, WRITE. The past tense words are FELL, RAN, SAW, SHOT, WROTE. You are to respond as quickly as possible whether the current word is present tense (press the / key) or past tense (press the z key). In other respects the experiment is similar to the shape experiment.

Gathering good data for this experiment requires that you become quite good at the classification experiment. There are at least 160 trials. If you incorrectly classify a stimulus, it will be presented again later. If you make mistakes often, slow down to ensure that you apply yourself to the classification task. You may find that you need to run this experiment several times to get good at the classification task. If you wish, before pressing the space bar, but after pressing the z or / key, you can check how many trials remain for the current experiment with the pull-down menu. You can also discard a trial, if you are distracted during its presentation, by pressing the t key instead of the z or / key. A discarded trial will be repeated later in the experiment. Remember to keep your eyes focused on the fixation point throught a trial. Do not move them to look at the shape or word, doing so will invalidate the experiment.

After the experiment a window will appear that summarizes your results. The data gives the average reaction time (RT) for four conditions: Shape left, Shape right, Word left, and Word right. Left and right correspond to the location of the stimulus on the screen, so the corresponding hemisphere in your brain is the flip (e.g., Left location -> Right hemisphere). Strong evidence for brain asymmetry would be found if Shape left RT was smaller than Shape right RT and Word left RT was larger than Word right RT. Not finding this type of data does not necessarily mean there is no asymmetry, but the statistical calculations needed to draw the conclusion are more complicated. The tests needed to test for brain asymmetry in those cases can be calculated using the trial-by-trial data.

Additional References

Chen, A. C., German, C. & Zaidel, D. W. (1997). Brain asymmetry and facial attractiveness: Facial beauty is not simply in the eye of the beholder. *Neuropsychologia* 35(4), 471-476.

Helland, T. & Asbjornsen, A. (2001) Brain asymmetry for language in dyslexic children. *Laterality, 6*(4), 289-301.

Hugdahl, K., Jorgensen, H. A. & Loberg, E. M. (2002). Functional brain asymmetry and attentional modulation in young and stabilized schizophrenic patients: A dichotic listening study. *Psychiatry Research, 109* (3), 281-299.

Robertson, L.C. (2003). The Asymmetrical Brain. *Journal of Cognitive Neuroscience, 15*(6), 921-922.

Schlang, G., Jancke, L., Huang, Y., & Steinmetz, H. (1995). In vivo evidence of structural brain asymmetry in musicians. *Science, 267,* 699-702.

Basic Questions

1. For an individual without brain damage, which of the scenarios should have a faster reaction time, the word DOG or a square displayed on the right hand side of a computer screen? Why?

2. When doing the CogLab, why was it important not to turn your head towards the stimulus being presented?

3. What general kind of information does the left hemisphere process? What about the right hemisphere?

4. When you are writing a creative story for your introductory English class, which hemisphere is most likely being activated? (Think about the creativity)

5. What is processed contralaterally in this lab if contralateral means opposite side?

Advanced Questions

1. Describe what kind of errors a split-brain patient would display if they were blindfolded and a banana was put in their left hand for naming?

2. How could you redesign this lab to test stimuli presented auditorily instead of visually? What would you expect your results to be for auditory information if brain asymmetry were present?

3. You are walking across campus, when you get hit on the right side of the head with a football because you did not duck in time. Use this lab to explain why this may not have occurred if it had come in on your left side.

Discussion Questions

1. Discuss the processing differences or problems of verbal material for a split-brain subject compared to a normal subject.

2. Discuss how this lab could be used in a clinical setting to compare normal processing with abnormal or problematic processing areas.

3.1 THE FEATURE APPROACH TO PERCEPTION

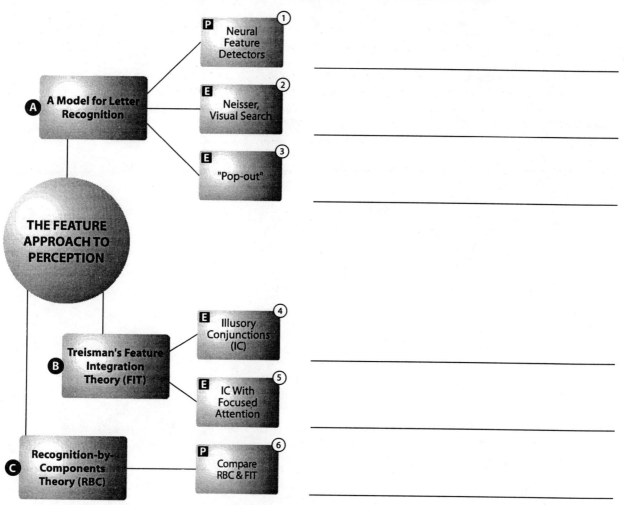

A What is the feature analysis model for recognizing letters?

① **Principle:** What is the neural mechanism for feature analysis? (64)

② **Experiment:** What is a visual search experiment? What did Neisser's experiment show, and how can his result be explained in terms of physiology? (Neisser; 65)

③ **Experiment:** What did Treisman's visual search experiment show? What is "pop out" and when does it occur? (Treisman, 66)

B What is Treisman's feature integration theory (FIT)?

④ **Experiment:** What are illusory conjunctions, how are they created, and what do they demonstrate about early visual processing? (Treisman, 68)

⑤ **Experiment:** What happened when Treisman repeated the illusory conjunction experiment, but had participants focus their attention on the target items? (Treisman, 70)

C What is Biederman's recognition-by-components (RBC) theory?

⑥ **Principle:** What does it mean to say that FIT and RBC theories explain two different facets of object perception? (73)

3.2 THE GESTALT APPROACH TO PERCEPTION

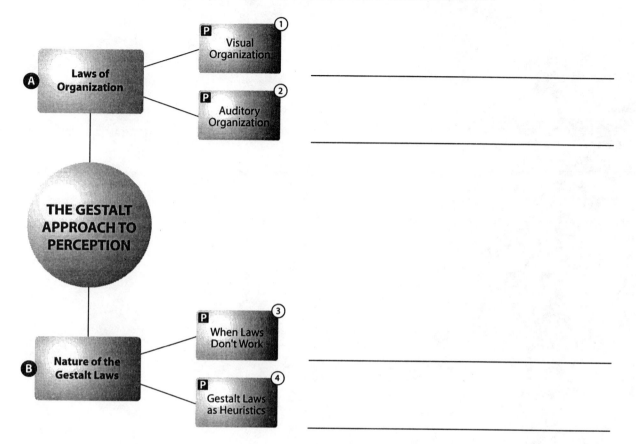

A What approach to perception was accepted in the early 1900's? Why can we say that the Gestalt approach was a reaction to that approach?

① **Principle:** Describe each of the Gestalt laws of organization, giving visual examples. (76)
② **Principle:** What is speech segmentation? What information do listeners use to achieve it? (80)

B What is the purpose of perception? What properties of the Gestalt laws help achieve this purpose?

③ **Principle:** Describe a situation in which application of the Gestalt laws results in an inaccurate perception of the environment. (81)
④ **Principle:** What is a heuristic? An algorithm? Why can we call the Gestalt laws heuristics? (82)

3.3 THE INTELLIGENCE OF OBJECT PERCEPTION

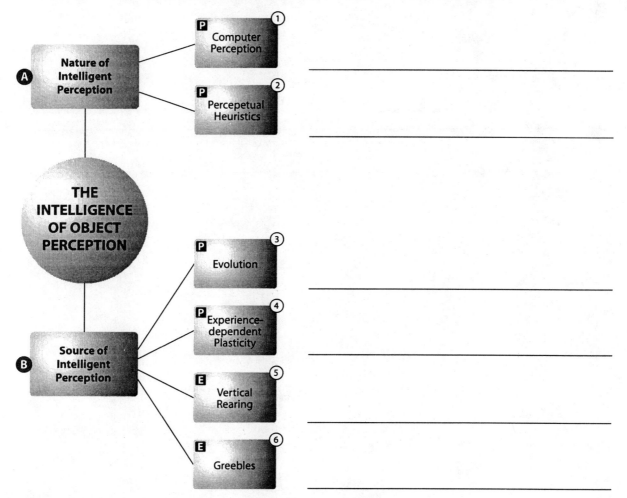

A Why can we say that even simple perceptions involve "intelligence"?

① **Principle:** Describe four reasons why computers have trouble perceiving objects. (83)

② **Principle:** Describe two heuristics, in addition to the Gestalt heuristics, that are associated with human perception. (87)

B What are the behavioral and physiological approaches to the question: Where does our perceptual intelligence come from?

③ **Principle:** How can evolution result in specialized neurons? (91)

④ **Principle:** What is experience-dependent plasticity? (91)

⑤ **Experiment:** What happens to a cat's cortical neurons if it is reared in an environment that consists only of verticals? (Blakemore & Cooper; 92)

⑥ **Experiment:** Describe the Greeble experiment. What does the result tell us about the adaptability of the brain? (Gauthier; 92)

Visual Search

This experiment explores aspects of attention in a visual search task. It is a classic experiment that makes strikingly clear the time needed to bring attention to bear on different regions of visual space. The basic idea is to ask a participant to search a visual image for a particular item and to respond as quickly as possible once they find the item, or to respond as quickly as possible when they are certain the item is not in the image. This type of experiment was used to develop a popular theory of attention (Treisman & Gelade, 1980).

Searches are divided into two types, those that require selective use of attention and those that do not. In the latter, the target item seems to "pop out" of the display and the participant can respond quickly. Notably, this pop out effect allows the participant to respond quickly even when the number of other (distractor) items is increased. In the other type of displays it seems that the participant is forced to study each item individually until the target item is found. In these cases the target item does not pop out, and search time increases with the number of distractor items. Controlling whether attention is needed or not is accomplished by the type of target and distractor items. In the experiment below, the target is always a green circle. For the feature condition the distractors are always blue squares. As you will see, the green circle seems to pop out of the image to quickly identify the location of the target. To require attention, the distractor items are made more complex. Some of the distractors are green squares while others are blue circles. Because some of the distractors are green, the green target circle no longer pops out and the participant must search through all the items to find the one that is both green and a circle. This type of search is a called conjunctive search because the target is a conjunction of features in the distractors.

For registration information go to http://coglab.wadsworth.com.

After clicking on the start button, a window will appear to start the feature search experiment. After positioning the mouse in the window press the space bar. A fixation dot will appear in the middle of the window, stare at it. A short time later (less than a second) circles and squares of various colors will appear on the screen. Your task is to determine if there is a green circle among the shapes. When you see a green circle, press the / key on your keyboard as quickly as possible. When you are certain there is not a green circle in the window, press the z key on your keyboard, again as quickly as possible.

After pressing the z or / key, press the space bar to start the next trial. If you wish, before pressing the space bar, but after pressing the z or / key, you can check how many trials remain for the current experiment with the pull-down menu.

The feature and conjunctive trials consist of approximately 48 trials each. If you make a mistake (e.g., say "Present" when you should have said "Absent") that trial is repeated later in the experiment, so you may actually run more than 48 trials. You can also discard a trial by pressing the t key instead of z or /. Discarding is appropriate if, after starting a trial, you sneeze, zone out, or are otherwise distracted.

31

Discarded trials will be repeated later.

In every trial your goal is simply to determine if a green circle is present. If it is press /, if it is not press z. If you are frequently incorrect (feedback is given when you are incorrect), try to delay your response until you are more certain that you are correct.

After you finish the set of feature search trials, the window will close and a new window will appear to present the conjunctive search trials.

After running both experiments a plot will appear that shows the time required for you to find the target ("Present" condition) or realize that the target was not there ("Absent" condition). These times will be plotted against "Number of distractors", which is the number of items on the screen. You should find that for the feature conditions changes in the number of distractors have little effect on search time. For the conjunctive searches you should find that search times increase with the number of distractors. You should also find that conjunctive "Absent" searches increase with the number of distractors at a faster rate than the conjunctive "Present" searches.

Additional References

D'Zmura, M. (1991). Color in Visual Search. *Vision Research, 31,* 951-966.

Findlay, J. M., & Gilchrist, I. D. (1998). Eye guidance and visual search. In G. Underwood (Ed.), *Eye Guidance in Reading and Scene Perception.* Amsterdam: Elsevier, 295-312.

Shih, S., & Sperling, G. (1996). Is there feature-based attentional selection in visual search? *Journal of Experimental Psychology: Human Perception & Performance, 22*(3), 758-779.

Wolfe, J. M. (1998). Visual Search. In H. Pashler (Ed.), *Attention.* Philadelphia: Taylor & Francis Press, 13-73.

Basic Questions

1. What is the "pop-out" effect? How is this related to visual perception?

2. What is a conjunctive search and how was it used in this lab?

3. Why do you think the reaction time for a conjunctive search should have been slower than for a feature search?

4. What happens to the reaction time in a conjunctive search as the number of distractors increases?

5. Your friend asks you to go out to her car in the mall parking lot to get her purse. She writes down her license plate number and tells you that her car is small and yellow and which entrance she used. Explain why this might take some time?

Advanced Questions

1. Humans make errors called conjunctive fallacies, where they believe that two events occurring at the same time has an increased probability of occurring than one event. Why do you think we make these errors? An example might help support your answer.

2. Why should it have taken more time in the conjunctive search to determine that a target was absent compared to the response time in determining the target was present?

Discussion Questions

1. Discuss how the visual search task helps to explain automatic and controlled visual processing.

2. Discuss how the number of distractors and the number of different features were related to the reaction time.

Apparent Motion

If two stimuli are briefly flashed in rapid succession, observers will sometimes report seeing motion between the two stimuli. Reports of this type of apparent motion were investigated near the beginning of the 20th century by Gestalt psychologists (most notably Wertheimer). They noticed, among other things, that the timing of the flashes was important in determining whether or not motion was seen. If the time between the offset of the first stimulus and the onset of the second stimulus (called the interstimulus interval or ISI) is very short, observers simply see two dots presented nearly simultaneously. If the ISI is very long observers see one dot flash on and off and then the other flash on and off. For intermediate ISIs the first dot seems to turn off, move through the space between the dots and appear at the position of the second dot.

Korte (1915) noted that the ISI thresholds for seeing motion versus being too short varied with the spatial separation of the stimuli. The farther apart the stimuli were the longer the ISI needed to be for a good motion percept. These findings, and others, were formulated in a set of "Korte's laws" that have been used to describe aspects of apparent motion.

The relationship between spatial separation and ISI threshold is consistent with a variety of theories that hypothesize that the visual system builds a motion percept. For larger separations, the stimulus must "move" a farther distance, which presumably requires a greater length of time. This experiment allows you to see apparent motion in one of its simplest forms and to demonstrate Korte's law for yourself.

Apparent motion is the basis of movement in all television, movies, and computer animation. The screen actually shows a rapid succession of still images, the perceived motion is entirely "apparent" and illusory.

For registration information go to http://coglab.wadsworth.com.

A window will fill the entire screen. Press the space bar key to start a trial. After pressing the space bar, a small fixation square will appear in the middle of the screen. Fixate this square. It will disappear after one and a half seconds. Half a second later a dot will appear on the right, disappear, and then a dot will appear on the left and disappear. These stimuli will then cycle back and forth repeatedly. Each of the dots is presented for 150 milliseconds; the duration of the blank between dots (the ISI) is variable.

Your task is to adjust the ISI until the motion percept is as strong as you can make it. You can increase the ISI by 20 milliseconds by pressing the i key. You can decrease the ISI by 20 milliseconds by pressing the k key. The ISI can never become negative.

After you are satisfied that the motion percept is as strong as you can make it, press the space bar to start the next trial. The spacing of the dots will vary from trial to trial. There are five spacings and five replications for each spacing, for a total of 25 trials.

At the end of the experiment a graph will appear that plots the average Best ISI (in milliseconds) as a function of distance from the center of the screen (the number is the proportion of screen width). You should find that the best ISI increases with distance. This would confirm some aspects of Korte's laws of apparent motion.

Additional References

Kaneoke, Y., Bundou, M., Koyama, S., Suzuki, H., & Kakigi, R. (1997). Human cortical area responding to stimuli in apparent motion. *Neuroreport, 8*, 677-682.

Kersten, D., Mamassian, P., & Knill, D. C. (1997) Moving cast shadows induce apparent motion in depth. *Perception, 26*(2), 171-192.

Mather, G. (1988). Temporal properties of apparent motion in subjective figures. *Perception, 17*, 729-736.

Morgan, M. J. (1992). Spatial filtering precedes motion detection. *Nature, 355*, 344-346.

Muckli, L., Kriegeskorte, N., Lanfermann, H., Zanella, F. E., Singer, W., & Goebel, R. (2002). Apparent motion: Event-related functional magnetic resonance imaging of perceptual switches and states. *Journal of Neuroscience, 22*(9), RC 219 (1-5).

Peterhans, E., & von der Heydt, R. (1991). Subjective contours: Bridging the gap between psychophysics and physiology. *Trends in Neurosciences, 14*, 112-119.

Basic Questions

1. What is the interstimulus interval or ISI?

2. Would your results agree with Korte's Law if the graph showed the interstimulus interval going from 43ms to 87ms to 122ms to 135ms to 205ms as the distance between the presented dots increased? Why?

3. How does this lab help to explain why the flashing arrow looks like it is pointing to the entrance of the university café?

4. Why do we perceive movement when we are watching television?

Advanced Questions

1. You are sitting on a bus looking out the window at another bus beside yours. As the other bus pulls away, you get the feeling that you are moving backwards. Explain what is going on.

2. You are watching a new Science fiction alien movie. You notice that the aliens do not move around like humans so; they seem to jump from one place to another. How do you think the film editors could have made it seem like they jumped from one place to another very quickly?

Discussion Questions

1. Discuss the relationship between the interstimulus interval and the distance between the objects as it relates to what is perceived by the viewer.

2. Discuss how designers of cartoons use the parameters of the apparent motion phenomenon when designing their sketches. How much time do you think is needed for the production of a 30-minute segment? Do you think the time of creation has reduced dramatically with computer programs?

Mapping the Blind Spot

The back of each of your eyes contains a dense set of receptors that are sensitive to light energy. These receptors convert light energy into electrical energy, which eventually is transferred to your nervous system and your brain. These receptors, however, are not distributed evenly across your eye. There is a central location, called the fovea, where the receptors are very densely packed. Generally, when you stare at an object you are arranging your eyes so that the object's image falls on the foveae of your eyes. Outside the fovea there are fewer receptors. In fact, in some places there are no receptors at all.

There is a place in each eye where the optic nerve exits the back of the eye to send information to the brain. This "hole" is called the optic disk. It contains no light sensitive receptors. As a result, any light that falls on this part of the eye is undetected and invisible to you. Functionally, this location on the eye is called the blind spot.

You have probably never noticed your blind spots (one in each eye). This is for several reasons. First, each blind spot is far away from its eye's fovea. Because the fovea is typically where you are "looking," you would not generally notice that something has disappeared into a blind spot. Second, when you view the world with two eyes, one eye can compensate for the other eye's blind spot. Light that falls into the blind spot of one eye generally does not fall on the blind spot of the other eye. Third, your brain only processes the presence of information, not the absence. Your brain does not notice a "hole" in the information it receives from the eye. It simply works with the information it receives. In a similar way, the brain does not observe that we are unable to view ultraviolet light. It has no knowledge about "missing" information.

With the proper experiment, however, it is possible to identify and map the blind spot, which is the purpose of this experiment. You will probably be surprised at how large the blind spot is. It covers a large part of your visual field. The experiment used here is similar to a test used by eye doctors to identify visual scotomas (damaged spots in the retina of your eye). Should you consistently find "holes" in your data other than the blind spot, you may want to see an eye doctor.

For registration information go to http://coglab.wadsworth.com.

A window will fill the entire screen. A small blue fixation square will be on the far left of the screen. The experiment is designed to map the blind spot of your right eye. Close your left eye (or cover it with your hand or a patch). Fixate the small square with your right eye. Try to sit so that your head is centered directly in front of the fixation square. Press the space bar key to start a trial. A dot will appear somewhere on the screen. Your task is to report whether you see the dot or not, all while keeping your right eye fixated on the small blue square.

If you see the dot, press the m-key. If you do not see the dot, press the n-key. Either of the keys you press will produce written feedback at the location of the fixation point. This is simply to indicate that the computer received your response. If the response is not what you intended (e.g., you pressed m when you meant to press n), just press the intended key. The computer will keep your last response as the response for that trial. Do not move your eye from the fixation square when you make this judgment. Press the space bar key to start the next trial when you are ready.

There are a total of 300 trials. That may sound like a lot, but each trial takes only a couple of seconds. You can take a break if you wish, but try to stay seated in the same position when you resume the experiment. If you move around, your blind spot will also move with you and the data will be a mix of the two positions you take. Also, be careful to make accurate judgments of whether you see or do not see the dot. If you try to go too fast, the computer will warn you to slow down. Most importantly, keep your right eye fixated on the small blue square. If you move your eye around, be sure to go back to the fixation square before making your judgment about seeing or not seeing a dot.

At the end of the experiment, you will be given two forms of data. First, the experimental window will show a full array of dots colored green and red. These dots are in the same locations you just viewed during the experiment. Any dot colored green is one that you reported as visible. Any dot colored red is one that you reported as not visible. You should find that there is a patch of red dots near the middle of the array. These are dots whose image fell on the blind spot of your eye. Its precise location varies a bit among observers and varies a lot depending on how far you are seated from the monitor. The same data is also presented in a data table in a separate window. Here 1's and 0's are used to indicate seen and not seen dots in the array, respectively.

Additional References

Brown, R. J. & Thurmond, J. B. (1993). Preattentive and cognitive effects on perceptual constancies at the blind spot. *Perception and Psychophysics, 53,* 200-209.

Dennett, D. C. (1991). *Consciousness explained.* Boston, MA: Little, Brown.

He, S., and Davis, W. (2001). Filling-in at the natural blind spot contributes to binocular rivalry. *Vision Research, 41,* 835-845.

Komatsu, H., Kinoshita, M. & Murakami, I. (2000). Neural responses in the retinotopic representation of the blind spot in the Macaque V1 to stimuli for perceptual filling-in. *Journal of Neuroscience, 20*(24), 9310-9319.

Tong, F., & Engel, S. A. (2001). Interocular rivalry revealed in the human cortical blind-spot representation. *Nature, 411,* 195-199.

Tong, F. (2003). Primary visual cortex and visual awareness. *Nature Reviews Neuroscience, 4,* 219-229.

1. What is another name for the blind spot? Why is it called the blind spot?

2. What kind of visual acuity do you have at the fovea?

3. In relation to the computer screen, where should the blind spot have been located?

4. If your results indicated no red spots anywhere in the matrix, would that mean that you don't have a blind spot?

5. You decide to dress up as a pirate for a Halloween dance. Why would it be a bad idea to drive to the dance with your patch on?

Advanced Questions

1. If you were a neurocognitive researcher, what would the blind spot evidence suggest about the brain's ability to adjust to the external environment?

2. In the Mapping the Blind Spot CogLab, you covered your left eye and stared at the target with your right eye. What side of the brain is processing most of this information?

Discussion Questions

1. Discuss why there is subjective variability in the results of this CogLab.

2. Explain how visually presented stimuli is processed through the eye and into the brain for processing.

Metacontrast Masking

Masking refers to a class of phenomena where presentation of one stimulus (the mask) can impair performance on some task that requires judgment about another stimulus (the target). Visual masking plays two roles in cognitive science. First, masking is used to investigate properties of the visual system. By identifying the way in which the target and mask stimuli influence each other, vision scientists are able to deduce details about the underlying mechanisms involved in visual perception. Second, visual masking is used to indirectly restrict systems involved in information processing of visual stimuli. The logic of this type of approach is that the mask can halt further processing of the target and one can thereby explore the order and time course of many information processing systems. A special subset of this approach is based on evidence that persons with various types of cognitive disorders may respond differently than normal people under some masking conditions. Thus, masking has been proposed as a simple method for detecting some disorders and as a means of specifying the underlying mechanisms for those disorders.

Both the target and mask stimuli are usually very brief (often less than 200 milliseconds). Despite its short duration, if the target stimulus is presented by itself, it is clearly visible and it is easy for observers to perform whatever judgment is required of them. What is interesting is that the subsequent presentation of a mask stimulus, even a hundred milliseconds after the target has turned off, can make the observer's task of judging something about the target exceedingly difficult. When this effect was first noted by Stigler (1910), it forced the field of perceptual psychology to realize that processing of visual information took time and could be interrupted. Backward masking has been used to identify details of the perceptual and cognitive processes involved in building percepts and judgments.

Metacontrast masking is a specific type of masking where the target and mask have no overlapping contours and the mask follows the target in time. A surprising finding in studies of metacontrast masking is that when performance on some judgment about the target is plotted against the interstimulus interval (ISI) between the target and mask, the resulting curve is u-shaped. Performance is generally quite good when the mask immediately follows the target. Performance is also generally good for very long (greater than 200 milliseconds) ISIs. For ISI between 60 and 100 milliseconds, however, performance is often quite poor. Some observers report that they do not see the target at all.

The effect of the mask on the target sometimes gets stronger as the target and mask are separated in time, which is contrary to many simple models of visual perception. Investigations of the u-shaped metacontrast masking function is numerous and has identified a variety of characteristics about the visual system.

For registration information go to http://coglab.wadsworth.com.

A window will fill the entire screen. Press the space bar key to start a trial. After pressing the space bar, a small fixation square will appear in the middle of the screen. Fixate this square. Half a second later four half dots (each like a half moon) will appear at the corners of an imaginary square around the fixation point. The half dots will be of random orientations. The dots will disappear after approximately 40 milliseconds. After a variable ISI, a mask annulus will appear at one of the corners of the imaginary square. Your task is to report the orientation of the half-dot that is at the same location as the mask annulus.

Make your selection by a key-press to indicate which side of the half-dot is missing. Press the i-key to indicate the top of the half dot is missing. Press the k-key to indicate the bottom of the half dot is missing. Press the j-key to indicate the left side of the dot is missing. Press the l-key to indicate the right side of the dot is missing. You can ignore all the other dots, only report on the dot at the same location as the masking annulus.

With each key-press, a half dot will appear that corresponds to the selection you are making. You can change your choice by pressing another key. When you are satisfied with your choice, press the space bar key to start the next trial. Before the next trial begins, you will be given feedback on whether your choice was correct. You will notice an error when the shown half dot corresponding to your choice changes to the actual orientation of the half dot.

The experiment varies the ISI between offset of the target half dots and the masking annulus. There are seven ISIs, and 30 trials for each ISI. This makes for a total of 210 trials. That may sound like a lot, but each trial only takes a few seconds, so the entire experiment will not take very long. Moreover, you can take a break between trials if needed. You should try your best to correctly identify the missing side of the half dot. Do not, however, be concerned if you make a lot of mistakes. The expected result is that for some ISIs identification of the half dot will be very difficult. It can make the task somewhat frustrating, though.

At the end of the experiment a graph will appear that plots the percent of correct identifications of the half dot as a function of interstimulus interval (ISI) between the target and mask in milliseconds. You should find that the curve is u-shaped, with the bottom at an ISI somewhere between 40 and 120 milliseconds.

Additional References

Eimer, M. (1999). Facilitatory and inhibitory effects of masked prime stimuli on motor activation and behavioural performance. *Acta Psychologica, 101,* 293-313.

Francis, G. (2000). Quantitative theories of metacontrast masking. *Psychological Review, 107*(4), 768-788.

Kirschfeld, K. & Kammer, T. (2000). Visual attention and metacontrast modify latency to perception in opposite directions, *Vision Research, 40,* 1027-1033.

Schlaghecken, F. & Eimer, M. (2001). Partial response activation to masked primes is not dependent on response readiness, *Perceptual and Motor Skills, 92,* 208-222.

1. After completing the Metacontrast Masking CogLab, what should your results graph look like? Why?

2. What is the independent variable? How many levels does this variable have? What are the specific levels?

3. Do you think that your perceptions would be more accurate if you answered quickly or thought about your answer first?

4. Do you think that your reaction time would be faster or slower if the target shape you had to respond to was in the same position as the previous response, for example, both in the upper right corner?

Advanced Questions

1. How is backwards masking used in Cognitive Psychology?

2. How is performance related to the interstimulus interval between the target and the mask?

Discussion Questions

1. Discuss why attention may be related to performance on this lab.

2. Discuss the role of the sensory store in memory.

Müller-Lyer Illusion

This experiment serves two purposes. First, it introduces a well known perceptual illusion called the Müller-Lyer illusion. Second, it demonstrates a psychophysical experimental method called the method of constant stimuli.

The Müller-Lyer illusion is easily demonstrated. In the figure below there are three horizontal lines. Two of the lines contain a pair of "wings." The wings are drawn outward or inward from the line ends. The illusion is that the line with the outward drawn wings tends to look longer than the line with the inward drawn wings. The line without wings tends to look smaller than the line with outward drawn wings and bigger than the line with inward drawn wings. It is an illusion because the lines are actually all the same length, which you can verify with a ruler.

This experiment is not directly about experiencing the illusion, which can be done just by looking at the figure, but is about using the illusion to demonstrate a common experimental technique: the method of constant stimuli.

It is fun to look at visual illusions and realize how our perception differs from reality. To guide the development of theories on cognition and perception, however, we need more specific data. We need to know, for example, just how long does the line with the wings drawn outward look? The more general question is, how do we measure characteristics of percepts? We cannot measure them directly because a percept is a particularly subjective experience.

The field of psychophysics deals with precisely this question. It attempts to relate reported characteristics of perception to physical properties. Instead of just asking an observer to look at and comment on stimuli, specific judgments are required and the stimuli are systematically varied. For the Müller-Lyer illusion, we will have observers compare the percept produced by a line with outward drawn wings to the percept produced by lines with no wings. We will systematically vary the length of the line without wings to see when the perceived line lengths match. We can then look at the physical length of the matching line without wings and use that as a measure of the strength of the Müller-Lyer illusion. There are several ways to go about making such comparisons. One of the simplest and most powerful is the method of constant stimuli. We will generate a large set of lines without wings of varying lengths and have the observer compare each one with a standard line with wings. For each comparison the observer notes whether the line without wings is perceived to be bigger or smaller than the line with wings. Unlike some other psychophysical methods (like the method of adjustment), the stimuli are not changeable by the observer, thus they are constant stimuli. The observer's task is just to report on the percept.

The goal of this type of experiment is to produce a psychometric function. That is a set of values that describes the probability of a certain response as a physical characteristic is varied. For the Müller-Lyer experiments, we will find the proportion of reports where the line without wings seemed bigger than the standard as a function of the physical length of the line without wings. With such a curve you can often identify critical values, such as the point of subjective equality, where the line without wings seemed to be the same size as the line with wings (e.g., 50% of the time it is described as bigger and 50% of the time is described as smaller).

For registration information go to http://coglab.wadsworth.com.

A window will fill the entire screen. Press the space bar key to start a trial. After pressing the space bar, two vertical lines will appear. The line on the lower right has outward drawn wings. The line on the upper left has no wings. Your task is to determine whether the line without wings is bigger or smaller than the line with wings. Press the i-key if the line without wings seems longer than the line with wings. Press the k-key if the line without wings seems shorter than the line with wings. Text will appear near the center of the screen with each key press to indicate that the computer has received your response. You can change your response if you wish. When you are satisfied with your response, press the space bar key to then start the next trial.

There are a total of 225 trials. Each trial only takes a few seconds to complete. Do not go too fast, though, or the computer will tell you to slow down and take time to make an accurate judgment of relative line lengths.

At the end of the experiment a graph will appear that plots the proportion of "Bigger" responses for different lengths of test lines (without wings). This is an approximation of the psychometric function. You should find that the proportion is zero on the far left of the plot and smoothly rises to the value one on the far right of the plot. On the y-axis find the location of the 0.5 mark. Go straight across horizontally to the plotted curve. Then go straight down to the x-axis. The length (in pixels) there is the perceived length of the line with wings. You should find that the number is larger than 100 (the actual length of the line with wings). That the number is larger than 100 is a quantitative description of the magnitude of the Müller-Lyer illusion.

Additional References

Anii, A., & Kudo, K. (1997). Effects of instruction and practice on the length-reproduction task using the Müller-Lyer figure. *Perceptual & Motor Skills, 85,* 819-825.

Di Maio, V., & Lansky, P. (1998). The Müller-Lyer Illusion in interpolated figures. *Perceptual & Motor Skills, 87,* 499-504.

Millar, S. & Al-Attar, Z. (2001). The Müller-Lyer Illusion in Touch and Vision: Implications for Multisensory Processes. *Perception & Psychophysics, 64*(3), 353-365.

Nelson, B. & Greene, E. (1998). Similar Müller-Lyer effects from operant and comparison response modes. *Perceptual & Motor Skills, 86,* 499-511.

Pollack, R. H. & Jaeger, T. (1991). Effect of lightness contrast on the colored Müller Lyer Illusion. *Perception & Psychophysics, 50,* 225-229.

Basic Questions

1. What does the magnitude of effect indicate about a person's judgment on the Müller Lyer Illusion?

2. How do you measure the magnitude of effect for the Müller Lyer Illusion? Give an example to support your answer.

3. Your psychology professor is trying to teach you about perceptual illusions. She takes an ordinary pencil and passes it around the room so everyone can feel that it is made of wood. When she gets the pencil back she wiggles it between her fingers and you swear it is moving like rubber. Why would this phenomenon be considered an illusion?

4. Your father wants to plant a tree in the yard but he is not sure what kind to put in. If he wants to plant a tree that gives the effect of being tall, what kind should he plant, a weeping willow or a maple? The maple tree has branches that grow upwards and a weeping willow has branches that grow downwards.

5. Here is another example of the Müller Lyer Illusion. Is it easier to detect the illusionary effect in the following example or the examples in the lab? Why?

Basic Questions

1. If you were told that the target line was not going to change in size, how would mental imagery help you in determining whether the test line was smaller or larger than the target line?

2. Look at the line below. Is this an example of the Müller Lyer Illusion? How would you know for sure?

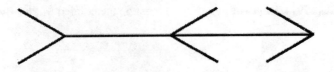

3. This CogLab used a psychophysical technique called the method of constant stimuli. What was held constant and why?

4. Describe how the Müller Lyer CogLab could be redesigned in terms of using a different psychophysical technique called the method of adjustment, meaning a participant is able to adjust the stimulus line, instead of the method of constant stimuli.

Discussion Questions

1. Discuss how illusions address the issue of contextual influences on perception and judgments.

2. Some research suggests that repeated trials of the Müller Lyer Illusion for the overall group, but individual differences may change drastically, meaning that the magnitude of effect may decrease for some people, while it increases for others. Discuss why you think this may occur. Think of external factors.

Signal Detection

Much of cognitive psychology involves gathering data from experimental participants. Gathering good data is not always easy, especially when one uses a variety of people as participants. Researchers must often carefully design an experiment to be certain participants are following the instructions and are motivated to try their best. Even despite these efforts, experimental results can be contaminated by individual differences if the researcher does not properly analyze the data.

For example, consider two participants in visual detection of a faint target. The researcher wants to explore a property of the visual system, so he/she presents a visual stimulus and asks the participants to report whether they saw the target. After 50 trials, participant A reports seeing the target 25 times and participant B reports detection 17 times. Did participant A do better? Not necessarily, perhaps participant A is simply more prone to report seeing the target and participant B is more conservative. That is, the two participants may have equivalent visual systems, but differences in reporting. Reports of simple detection do not allow the researcher to compare participants' results.

A better experiment is a modification of the one above. Have two kinds of trial, one with the target present and one with the target absent. Again have subjects report whether they saw the target. There are four statistics to be calculated from this experiment. Trials where a participant correctly detects the target are called hits. The trials where the target was there but participants did not detect it are called misses. If a participant reports seeing the target when it was not actually there, he/she has made a mistake (false alarm). A trial where the participant correctly reports that the target was not present is a correct rejection.

Suppose that after 100 trials (50 for target present and 50 for target absent) the researcher again finds that on the trials where the target was in fact present, participant A reports seeing it 25 times and participant B 17 times. Who is doing better? It depends on the frequency of false alarms. If participant A has 25 false alarms and participant B has 5 false alarms, then B is better than A at distinguishing the trials where the target is present from the trials where the target is absent. That is, in this case, A seems to often guess that the target is there, but he/she is wrong (false alarm) as often as right (hit). B is more selective about saying he/she detects the target, but rarely says the target is there when it is not. Thus, B is doing better.

This type of analysis suggests that you need to consider two numbers, hits and false alarms to really be able to compare performance across subjects. Fortunately, one can combine the numbers in a careful way to produce a single number that gives an indication of the sensitivity of the participant to the presence of the target. The calculation is structured so that, with certain assumptions, it will not matter whether a participant takes a conservative or liberal approach to claiming to detect the target. There are two measures of sensitivity that are often used. One is called d' (d-prime) and is based on signal detection theory. The other is called log(alpha) and is based on choice theory. For most situations the two measures give very similar results, although there are quantitative differences.

A discussion of the algorithms for calculating sensitivity is beyond the scope of this experiment [see

Macmillan & Creelman, (1991) for further discussion]. Instead, you will participate in an experiment that measures sensitivity.

For registration information go to http://coglab.wadsworth.com.

After clicking on the start button, a window will appear that fills the screen. Press the space bar to start a trial. After pressing the bar a fixation point will appear for a second or so and then will be replaced by randomly placed dots (sort of like a "star field"). On some trials (target present) an additional set of ten dots arranged in a straight line that slants downward from left to right is randomly placed among the dot field. On the other trials (target absent), the line is not included. Your task is to report whether the target is present or absent.

If you think the target is present, press the / key. If you think the target is not present, press the z key. You will be given feedback on whether you were correct. In addition, on the trials where the target was actually present, a green line will connect the target dots after you make your decision. Look for the dots along this line so you will learn what the target looks like; but the target will be randomly placed on the screen from trial to trial. There are a total of 60 trials. Thirty with the target line present and thirty with the target line absent.

When the experiment finishes the window will close and a new window will appear with data on your performance. The data will include several statistics:
- HITS: the percentage of times you said you detected the target and it was actually there.
- FALSE ALARMS: the percentage of times you said you detected the target, but the target was not actually present.
- CORRECT REJECTIONS: the percentage of times you said you did not detect the target, and the target was not actually present.
- MISSES: the percentage of times you said you did not detect the target, but it was actually there.

The data will also report a sensitivity statistic called d' (pronounced dee-prime). The program uses a method proposed by Brophy (1986) to compute d'. The larger the d' value, the better your performance. A sensitivity value of zero means that you cannot distinguish trials with the target from trials without the target. A sensitivity of 4.6 indicates a nearly perfect ability to distinguish between trials that included the target and trials that did not include the target. Values between these extremes correspond to intermediate sensitivity to the target. (Negative sensitivities are possible, but will be close to zero unless you misunderstood the instructions.) You will also see the signal detection measure of response bias, C (see Snodgrass & Corwin, 1988). A value greater than 0 indicates a conservative bias (a tendency to say `absent' more than `present') and a value less than 0 indicates a liberal bias. Values close to 0 indicate neutral bias.

You can repeat the experiment several times, and intentionally vary your approach to making responses. For one experiment you could take a very conservative approach and only report that you see the target if you are very certain. One another session of the experiment you could take a looser approach and report that you see the target unless you are certain it is not there. You should find that your sensitivity score does not change very much, even though your bias score will vary substantially.

Additional References

Bonnel, A., Mottron, L., Peretz, I., Trudel, M., Gallun, E. & Bonnel, A. (2003). Enhanced pitch sensitivity in individuals with autism: A signal detection analysis. *Journal of Cognitive Neuroscience, 15*, 226-235.

Erev, I., Gopher, D., Itkin, R. & Greenshpan, Y. (1995). Toward a generalization of Signal Detection Theory to n-person games: The example of two person safety problem. *Journal of Mathematical Psychology, 39*, 360-376.

Gable, S., Reis, H., & Downey, G. (March, 2003). He said, she said: A quasi-signal detection analysis of daily interactions between close relationship partners. *Psychological Science, 14*(2), 100-103.

Hu, X. & Ahuja, N. (1994). Feature extraction and matching as signal detection. *International Journal of Pattern Recognition and Artificial Intelligence, 8*(6), 1343-1379.

Wickens, T. D. (2002). *Elementary Signal Detection Theory.* Oxford, England: Oxford.

Basic Questions

1. Let's say that you have completed the lab and you get a "C" value of 1.39, what does this suggest about your response bias?

2. If you have a conservative bias, which signal detection errors would be higher, false alarms or misses?

3. A good friend of yours just had a baby. When detecting if the baby is crying or not, what error would she make more often-false alarms or misses? Why?

4. Your professor is very hard on people who make spelling errors on tests and assignments. Every time you make a spelling error, she circles it in bright red pen and she points it out to the class. What kind of signal detection errors would you make when you are checking for spelling errors on your test? Why?

5. One night you are at a sorority function when you think this guy is checking you out from across the room. If you walk over and talk to him, thinking he is interested in you, but he walks away and starts talking to the girl who was standing behind you, what kind of detection error did you make?

1. You are a manager in a factory that makes widgets. Lately, Bob is making poor quality widgets, but he tells you that they didn't notice problems with his widgets when they packaged them. What kind of error did Bob make in the detection of product errors? How could you increase Bob's attention to the quality of his widgets?

2. Military radar is used as an automatic early detection system for stimuli that should not be there, like missiles or enemy invasion. What kind of problems could you foresee in errors such as false alarms and misses? How could the enemy use this knowledge to their benefit?

Discussion Questions

1. Discuss how to decrease false alarms in social behaviors. In your answer, talk about how decreasing false alarms would affect the other 3 scenarios (Hits, Misses and Correct Rejections).

2. How is vigilance related to signal detection and the sensitivity index that was calculated in the lab?

4.1 SELECTIVE ATTENTION I

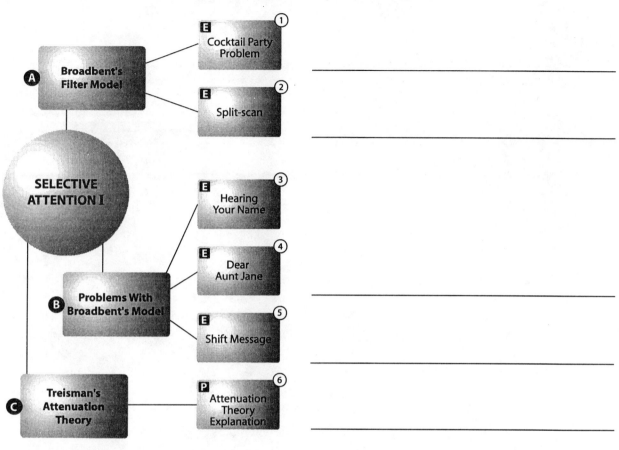

(A) **What is Broadbent's filter model of attention?**

① **Experiment:** Describe the dichotic listening experiment that led to Broadbent's filter model. (Cherry; 102)

② **Experiment:** What was the "split-scan" experiment and what did it demonstrate, according to Broadbent? (Broadbent; 104)

(B) **What point do all three experiments below make about how information is processed in the unattended ear?**

③ **Experiment:** What happens when a person's name is presented to the unattended ear in a dichotic listening experiment? (Moray; 105)

④ **Experiment:** What was the "Dear Aunt Jane" experiment and what did it demonstrate? (Gray & Wedderburn; 105)

⑤ **Experiment:** Describe the experiment in which the message was shifted from one ear to another. (Treisman; 106)

(C) **Why was an alternative to Broadbent's filter model needed?**

⑥ **Principle:** How does Treisman's attenuation theory explain why we can sometimes hear "important" messages such as our name, even if we are not attending to them? (106)

4.2 SELECTIVE ATTENTION II

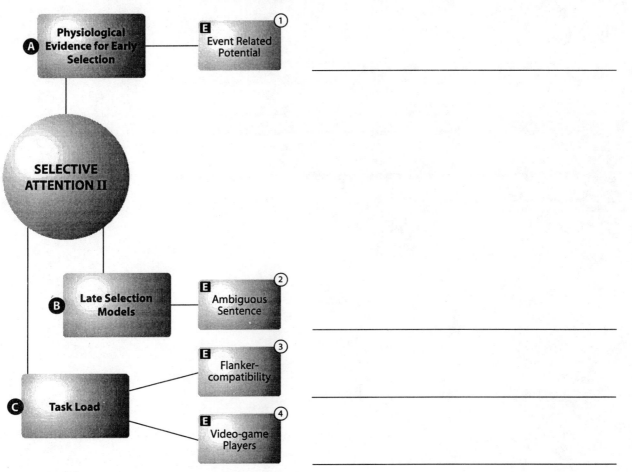

A   **What is the event-related potential (ERP), and what can its different waves tell us?**

①   **Experiment:** Describe the ERP experiment that provides evidence for early selection. (Hillyard; 108)

B   **When does selection occur, according to the late selection models?**

②   **Experiment:** Describe the "throwing stones at the bank" experiment. How does the result support late selection theory? (MacKay; 109)

C   **What are Lavie's predictions about the effect of task load on selection?**

③   **Experiment:** What is the flanker-compatibility task? Describe the experiment in which participants were asked to decide if one of the shapes was a square or a diamond. How was task load varied, and how did varying task load affect performance? (Green & Bavelier; 110)

④   **Experiment:** Describe the experiment in which experienced video-game players were presented with the same flanker-compatibility task as above. How were their results different from the results of inexperienced players? (Green & Bavelier; 111)

4.3 DIVIDED ATTENTION

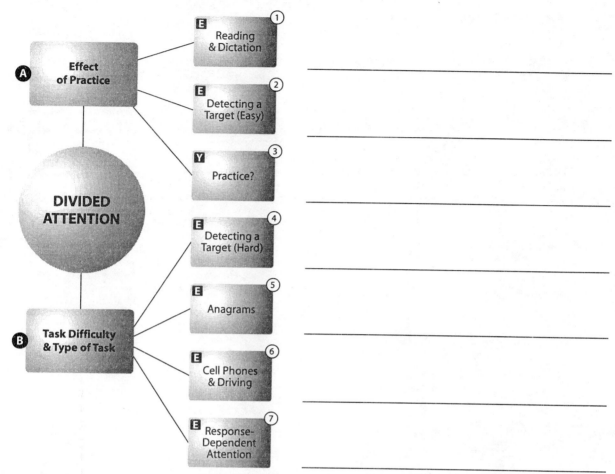

A What is divided attention and when is it possible?

① **Experiment:** Describe the experiment that involved reading and responding to dictation simultaneously. (Spelke; 113)

② **Experiment:** Describe the experiment that involved indicating when a target from a "memory set" was present in a series of "frames". What happened after about 600 trials? (Schneider & Shiffrin; 113). What happened to performance if the number of characters was increased? (113)

③ **Your Experience:** Describe one or two tasks you have practiced so much that you use automatic processing to accomplish them.

B How does task difficulty and the type of task affect the ability to attend to more than one thing at once?

④ **Experiment:** Describe the second part of the experiment in 2, above. Be sure you understand the difference between consistent mapping and varied mapping. Describe the difference between automatic processing and controlled processing. (Schneider & Shiffrin; 116)

⑤ **Experiment:** Describe the anagram experiment. What does the result illustrate about divided attention? (Tyler; 117)

⑥ **Experiments:** What did the Toronto study of traffic accidents and cell phone use show? (Hafner). What did the simulated driving experiment show? (Strayer & Johnston; 118)

⑦ **Experiment:** Describe the experiment that involved dividing attention between visual and verbal tasks. What do the results demonstrate about the effect of pairing tasks (visual-verbal; visual-visual; verbal-verbal) on divided attention? (Brooks; 119)

4.4 VISUAL ATTENTION

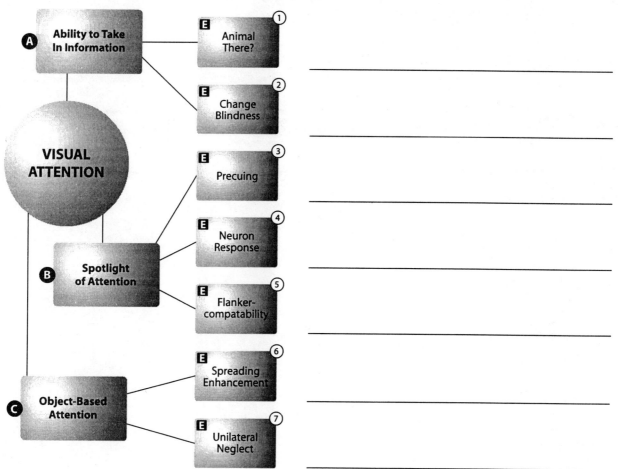

A How well can people take in information from brief presentations of visual stimuli?

① **Experiment:** Describe the experiment in which participants had to pay attention to letters and indicate what was in a photograph presented off to the side. (Li; 120)

② **Experiments:** What is change blindness? What does it demonstrate about our ability to attend to details of a scene? (Rensink; Levin; 120)

B What is the spotlight model of attention?

③ **Experiment:** Describe the precuing procedure. How does the result of the precuing experiment support the spotlight model? (Posner; 124)

④ **Experiment:** Describe the experiment that measured the response of a neuron in the monkey's cortex in "attention" and "no attention" conditions. (Colby; 125)

⑤ **Experiment:** Describe the flanker-compatibility experiment. How does the result support the spotlight model? (Eriksen & Eriksen; 126)

B What is object-based attention?

⑥ **Experiment:** Describe the experiment in which participants were cued to where on a rectangle a target might appear. Why does the result support the idea of object-based attention? (Egly; 128)

⑦ **Experiment:** Describe the experiment in which a patient with unilateral neglect was told to pay attention to targets presented in a "barbell" stimulus. How does the result demonstrate object-based attention? (Tipper & Behrmann; 130)

Spatial Cueing

The "spotlight" metaphor of visual attention nicely captures many characteristics of the focus of attention: it is a "beam" that is moved spatially, that may not be divided, and that enhances the detection of events falling within it.

Some of the strongest evidence supporting the unitary conception of attention comes from the luminance-detection paradigm (e.g., Posner, 1980). In such experiments, subjects are first cued with the likely spatial location of a target and then respond as rapidly as possible when the target appears at any location in the display. For example, in a typical display, the stimuli are arranged horizontally with a fixation point in the center, which is also the location where the cue appears. The cue is either valid, correctly identifying the spatial location of the target, or invalid, incorrectly identifying the location of the target. Following the presentation of the cue, a single target stimulus is illuminated (usually about 1000 ms after the onset of the cue) and subjects respond as soon as they detect the target, regardless of its location. Relative to a neutral cue condition, responses are faster when the target appears in the cued location (a valid trial) and slower when the target appears in a non-cued location (an invalid trial).

Demonstrations of these patterns of results occur independently of eye movements. In other words, when an eye tracker verifies that your eyes are still fixated on the center, your focus of attention can be off to the right, or off to the left. While other interpretations of these findings are possible, they are consistent with the notion of focused beam of attention that may be moved to distinct spatial locations - incorrectly in the case of the an invalid trial and correctly in the case of a valid trial.

For registration information go to http://coglab.wadsworth.com.

After clicking on the start the button, a window will appear to start the experiment. Start a trial by pressing the space bar. A fixation dot will appear in the middle of the window; stare at it. A short time later a cue will appear. If the arrow points to the right, 80% of the time the target will appear on the right. If the arrow points to the left, 80% of the time, the target will appear on the left. If no arrow appears, the target is equally likely to appear on the left or right. A short time after the cue disappears, a red square will appear. Your task is to respond as quickly as possible when you see the square appear, regardless of its location. To respond, press the n key.

After pressing the n key, press the space bar to start the next trial. If you wish, before pressing the space bar, but after pressing the n key, you can check how many trials remain for the current experiment with the pull-down menu.

There are 80 trials. You can discard a trial by pressing the t key instead of n. Discarding is appropriate if, after starting a trial, you sneeze, zone out, or are otherwise distracted. Discarded trials will be repeated later.

In every trial your goal is simply to press the n key as soon as you see a red square appear.

At the end of the experiment a new window will appear that reports the reaction time in milliseconds for detecting the square in each of the conditions. The neutral condition provides a baseline measure when your attention is not cued. The expected result is that RTs in the valid condition (the arrow cue pointed to the correct location) will be faster than those in the neutral condition (a benefit) whereas RTs in the invalid condition (the arrow cue pointed to the wrong location) will be slower than those in the neutral condition (a cost).

Additional References

Atchley, P. & Kramer, A. (1998). Spatial cueing in a stereoscopic display: Attention remains "depth-aware" with age. *Journal of Gerontology: Psychological Sciences, 53*, 318-323.

Egly, R., Driver, J. & Rafal, R. D. (1994). Shifting visual attention between objects and locations: Evidence from normal and parietal lesion subjects. *Journal of Experimental Psychology: General, 123*, 161-177.

Eriken, C. W. & Yeh, Y (1985). Allocation of attention in the visual field. *Journal of Experimental Psychology: Human Perception and Performance, 11*, 583-597.

Luck, S., Hillyard, S., Mouloua, M., Woldorff, M., Clark, V. & Hawkins, H. (1994). Effects of spatial cueing on luminance detectability: Psychophysical and electrophysiological evidence. *Journal of Experimental Psychology, Human Perception and Performance, 20*, 887-904.

Posner, M. I. & Cohen, Y. (1984). Components of visual orienting. In H. Bouma & D. G. Bouwhuis (Eds.). *Attention and Performance.* Hillside, NJ: Erlbaum

Basic Questions

1. When examining the results of the lab, which of the three reaction times were lower (faster) - (a) no cue (b) valid cue or (c) invalid cue? If the "no cue" reaction time was faster than the invalid cue, what could be inferred about invalid cues?

2. How does a ventriloquist use spatial cues to direct a person's attention away from him and towards his dummy or doll?

3. While exploring a cave, you hear screeching echoes that you believe are bats (not one of your favorite animals). What will happen to your reaction time if you try to escape the bats in this cave?

4. You are playing a video game where you place oddly shaped playing pieces into a game area as quickly as possible. The object is to form solid rows with these shapes to make the rows disappear because if there is a space, the row does not disappear. Just 0.5 seconds before a shape appears, a dot flashes on the side where it will come down from. However, as the game advances, you notice that

sometimes the dots are on the wrong side as the shape. How do you think these miscues will affect your game?

5. You are playing your final game against York University, a strong offensive team. You are defending number 23, a top player and well known for his fancy footwork. Why does he beat you to the basket every time after he fakes his body to the right but then goes left? Explain in terms of your reaction speed to his moves.

Advanced Questions

1. In Classical Conditioning, effective learning of an association is diminished when the unconditioned stimulus and the conditioned stimulus are not paired closely together in time. How is this similar to something that could happen when presented with invalid cues?

2. How are cognitive expectations related to one's reaction time to a stimulus?

3. How might an animal, in its natural environment, use techniques to misinform a predator of its location?

Discussion Questions

1. How do you think directors of horror movies use invalid spatial cues to their advantage when the good guys are trying to get away from the bad guys (especially when a chainsaw is involved)?

2. In terms of conserving energy, why do animals, including humans, use heuristics or short cuts in cognitive tasks, since heuristics may be incorrect? When explaining your answer, think of this lab as well as others that you have done or other cognitive processes that you've talked about in class.

Stroop Effect

When you first learned to tie shoelaces you needed to carefully think through each step of the process. Now, you probably do not even seem to think about the steps, but simply initiate a series of movements that seem to proceed without any further influence. When a behavior or skill seems to no longer require direct interaction, cognitive psychologists say it is automatized.

Many behaviors can become automatized: typing, reading, writing, bicycling, piano playing, driving, etc. Automatization is interesting because it is an important part of daily life. We perform a variety of automatized behaviors quickly and effortlessly. In some cases people report that they do not consciously know how the behavior is performed, they just will it to happen, and it does happen.

To explore properties of automatized behaviors cognitive psychologists often put observers in a situation where an automatized response is in conflict with the desired behavior. This allows researchers to test the behind-the-scenes properties of automatized behaviors by noting their influence on more easily measured behaviors. This demonstration explores a well-known example of this type of influence, the Stroop effect.

Stroop (1935) noted that observers were slower to properly identify the color of ink when the ink was used to produce color names different from the ink. That is, observers were slower to identify red ink when it spelled the word blue. This is an interesting finding because observers are told to not pay any attention to the word names and simply report the color of the ink. However, this seems to be a nearly impossible task, as the name of the word seems to interfere with the observer's ability to report the color of the ink.

A common explanation for the Stroop effect is that observers (especially college undergraduates) have automatized the process of reading. Thus, the color names of the words are always processed very quickly, regardless of the color of the ink. On the other hand, identifying colors is not a task that observers have to report on very often, and because it is not automatized it is slower. The fast and automatic processing of the color name of the word interferes with the reporting of the ink color.

The Stroop task, and its many variations, is a commonly used tool in cognitive psychology to explore how different types of behaviors interact. This demonstration allows you to participate in a simple version of the Stroop task.

For registration information go to http://coglab.wadsworth.com.

After clicking on the start the button, a window will appear to start the experiment. Start a trial by pressing the space bar. A fixation dot will appear in the middle of the window, stare at it. A short time later (less than a second) a word (RED, GREEN, or BLUE) will appear on the screen, and the word will be drawn in red, green, or blue font color. Your task is to classify, as quickly as possible, the font color, regardless of the word name. If the font color is red, press the h key; for green, press the j key; for blue, press the k key. It may take a bit of practice to make certain you remember which key corresponds to which font color.

After pressing a key to identify the font color, you will receive feedback on whether you were correct. If you were incorrect the trial will be repeated later in the experiment. If you find you are making lots of mistakes you should slow down, or make certain you understood which key goes with which font color. Press the space bar to start the next trial. If you wish, before pressing the space bar, but after identifying the font color, you can check how many trials remain for the current experiment with the pull-down menu.

There are at least 45 trials, 30 where the font colors and word names are different and 15 where the font colors and color names match (e.g., the word RED in red font color). You can also discard a trial by pressing the t key instead of identifying the font color. Discarding is appropriate if, after starting a trial, you sneeze, zone out, or are otherwise distracted. Discarded trials will be repeated later.

At the end of the experiment a new window will appear that reports the reaction time in milliseconds for identifying the font color when the word names and colors match and when they are different. You should find that the reaction time is longer when the word names and colors are different.

Additional References

Cohen, J. D., Dunbar, K. & McClelland, J. L. (1990). On the control of automatic processes: A parallel distributed processing account of the Stroop effect. *Psychological Review, 97* (3), 332-361.

Cox, C. S., Chee, E., Chase, G. A., Baumgardner, T. L., Schuerholz, L. J., & Reader, M. J. (1997). Reading proficiency affects the construct validity of the Stroop test interference score. *Clinical Neuropsychologist, 11*, 105-110.

Davidson, D. J, Zacks, R. J., & Williams, C. C. (2003). Stroop interference, practice, and aging. *Aging Neuropsychology and Cognition, 10*, (2) 85-98.

MacLeod, C. M. (1991). Half a century of research on the Stroop effect: An integrative review. *Psychological Bulletin, 109*, 163-203.

MacLeod, C. M., & Bors, D. A. (2002). Presenting two color words on a single Stroop trial: Evidence for joint influence, not capture. *Memory & Cognition, 30*, 789-797.

Basic Questions

1. What was the independent variable in this experiment? What are the levels of the independent measure? What was the dependent variable? How was the dependent variable measured?

2. In this experiment, if you made an error, that trial was repeated later. How could you change the dependent measure in this experiment so that this did not occur?

3. Jim works in a glass recycling plant and is responsible for sorting the colored glass into the different bins for processing. Jim is thankful for this job because he only has a grade 9 education. How do you think Jim would do on the Stroop test? Explain your answer.

4. Do you think that practice would decrease the Stroop effect?

5. Do you think that the Stroop effect would be present in individuals who weren't fluent readers? Why or why not?

Advanced Questions

1. How could the Stroop test be used in clinical psychology to identify phobias, for example if Joe is afraid of spiders?

2. What would you expect the results of a Stroop test to be for a bilingual person? Do you think that the Stroop effect would be equal for both languages? Explain your answer.

3. Explain how automatization is related to the Stroop effect. Use the variables of this lab to help explain your answer.

Discussion Questions

1. You can see how the Stroop test is used in clinical psychology, as shown in the above question. In what other ways could the Stroop test be used as pre-and post-tests or as general tests of cognitive ability or alertness in clinical and applied psychology?

2. How do you think older adults perform on the Stroop test compared to younger adults? Explain your answer in terms of cognitive processing.

Attentional Blink

Cognitive mechanisms can handle only limited amounts of information. In many situations there are more stimuli and mental events than resources for processing. As a result, some stimuli are processed and some are not. The ability to selectively choose some stimuli and ignore others is called attention. Many studies of attention investigate how mental resources are switched from one stimulus to another. This experiment explores some properties of attention with rapidly changing stimuli. It shows that there is a brief time after paying attention to one stimulus where attention cannot be focused on a subsequent stimulus. This duration is called an attentional blink because it is analogous to being unable to see objects during an eye blink.

In the experiment many letters are shown in rapid succession, with each letter overwriting the previous letter. The observer's task is to watch the entire sequence, and then indicate whether certain target letters were in the sequence. The sequences are carefully constructed to systematically vary the temporal separation between two target letters. Thus, if the target letters are J and K, a sequence with the letters ". . . JXTVRK . . ." places K five letter-spaces beyond J.

The notable finding is that identification of the second target letter is very low when it quickly follows the first target letter. As temporal separation increases, identification of the second letter improves. This finding suggests that when the observer sees the first target letter he/she must attend to it to ensure that it will be remembered later. The focusing of attention to that letter apparently requires time, and if the second target letter appears during that time, it is not attended and not reported. By looking at recognition of the second letter as a function of separation, we can estimate the time required to focus and break attention for stimuli.

As a final note, although the task in this experiment may seem rather absurd, it is quite similar to tasks some individuals must perform on a routine basis. In the airline industry both pilots and controllers attend to many different stimuli that change characteristics very quickly. The temporal properties of attention revealed through studies like this one help guide development of more general theories of attention, with immediate applications to high-pressure situations. This experiment allows you to participate in a version of an attentional blink experiment.

For registration information go to http://coglab.wadsworth.com.

Start a trial by pressing the space bar. A sequence of 19 letters will appear, with each new letter overwriting the previous one. Each letter is presented for only 100 milliseconds. Your task is to determine whether the letter J and/or K were in the sequence of letters just presented. You indicate the presence of a J by pressing the j key and you indicate the presence of the K by pressing the k key. If you see both letters, press each in any order. If you did not see either letter, do not press either key. The screen will present the key you press, but this is only so you know the program received your key press; it is not feedback on whether you were correct. When you are ready for the next trial, press the space bar again.

If for some reason you need to discard a trial (e.g., you sneezed, attention drifted, you "zoned out", et cetera) press the t key before pressing the space bar for the next trial. This will discard the just run trial (it will be re-run later in the experiment).

When you finish the experiment, a window will appear that plots the percentage of times you detected the first and second target letters as a function of separation. You should find that the second target is detected more frequently as separation increases. You should also find that the detection of the first target is relatively unaffected by separation. This finding supports the hypothesis that bringing attention to the first target interferes with detection of the second, but not vice-versa. A separation equal to zero corresponds to a sequence where only the first letter was presented. You should find that, for separation zero, detection frequency for the second target is zero.

There are 100 trials in the experimental session. There are five letter separations, with 20 sequences for each separation. Each trial goes very quickly, so the experiment will probably not take more than half an hour. It will be a tiring half-hour, however, as you must apply yourself to the task of watching the rapid letter sequences.

Additional References

Arnell, K. M. & Jolicoeur, P. (1999). The attentional blink across stimulus modalities: Evidence for central processing limitations. *Journal of Experimental Psychology: Human Perception and Performance, 25*, 630-648.

Deco, G. & Schurmann, B. (2000). A Neuro-cognitive visual system for object recognition based on testing of interactive attentional top-down hypotheses. *Perception and Psychophysics, 29*, 1249-1264.

Kranczioch, C., Debener, S. & Engel, A. K. (2003). Event-related potential of the attentional blink phenomenon. *Cognitive Brain Research, 17*, 177-187.

Lawson, M. L., Crewther, S. G., Kiely, P. M., & Crewther, D. P. (2001). Development of the attentional blink in relation to cognitive and short-term memory development. *Journal of Vision, 1*(3), 218.

Ross, N. N. & Jolicoeur, P. (1995). Attentional blink for color. *Journal of Experimental Psychology: Human Perception and Performance, 25*, 1483-1494.

Shapiro, K., Driver, J., Ward, R., & Sorensen, R. E. (1997). Priming from the Attentional Blink: A failure to extract visual tokens but not visual types. *Psychological Science, 8*, 95-100.

Basic Questions

1. What cognitive process is a researcher studying when he is interested in a person's ability to selectively choose some stimuli while ignoring other stimuli?

2. Assume the theory of attentional blink is correct. Describe what your results graph of percent reported vs. separation should look like for the first target and second target.

3. You are driving to school singing along to the radio, when you are startled by something running across the road. When you look back into your mirror, you see two squirrels were trying to cross the road. If you only saw one squirrel, how could this CogLab help to explain why you didn't see the other one?

Advanced Questions

1. What two methodological changes could you make to increase your chance of seeing the second target?

2. Use the plot of the mean, detected as a function of separation, to estimate how long an attentional blink lasts in the demonstration. (Hint: remember that each letter is presented for 100 milliseconds.)

Discussion Questions

1. Discuss why the attentional blink might be a hindrance for some animals or humans that live in a complex world. Think in terms of survival.

2. Discuss how attention is related to long-term memory.

Simon Effect

The Simon effect refers to the finding that people are faster and more accurate responding to stimuli that occur in the same relative location as the response, even though the location information is irrelevant to the actual task (Simon, 1969). Studying the Simon effect gives us insight into a stage of decision making called "response selection." According to information processing theory, there are three stages of decision making: Stimulus identification, response selection and response execution or the motor stage.

Superficially, the Simon effect may seem similar to the Stroop effect. However, it is generally accepted that the interference that occurs in the Stroop effect comes from the stimulus identification, while the interference that occurs in the Simon effect occurs in the response selection stage. During response selection, a person uses a rule to translate the relevant stimulus dimension, usually shape or color, to the correct left or right response. However, the location dimension of the stimulus (its position on the screen) overlaps with the relevant stimulus dimension (left or right). Because of this, the irrelevant location dimension of the stimulus activates the corresponding response and interferes with making a response to the non-corresponding side. Because of this, same side responses are faster and more accurate than responses that are made opposite the location of the stimulus.

In the real world the Simon effect has important implications. Primarily, it shows that location information cannot be ignored, and will affect decision making, even if the user knows that the information is irrelevant. The Simon effect (and related phenomena) must be taken into account in design of man-machine interfaces. Good interfaces display information in ways that match the types of responses people should make. For example, imagine that you are flying a plane, and the left engine has a problem. The indicator for that engine should be to the left of a corresponding indicator for the right engine. If it is the other way around, you may misrespond to the indicator and adjust the wrong engine. That could be problematic.

For registration information go to http://coglab.wadsworth.com.

After clicking on the start button, a window will appear to start the Simon effect experiment. Press the space bar to start the trial. A fixation dot will appear in the middle of the window, stare at it. A short time later (less than a second) you will be shown a red or green square on the left or right of fixation. Your task is to press the m key if the square is green and to press the v if the square is red. Keep your left index finger on the v, and your right index finger on the m. You will need to press the spacebar to start a new trial. After each trial, you will be given feedback whether your response was correct or incorrect, and how fast your reaction time was, in milliseconds.

After pressing the v or m key, press the space bar to start the next trial. If you wish, before pressing the space bar, but after pressing the v or m key, you can check how many trials remain for the current experiment with the pull-down menu.

There are 100 trials. You can discard a trial by pressing the t key instead of v or m. Discarding is appropriate if, after starting a trial, you sneeze, zone out, or are otherwise distracted. Discarded trials will be repeated later.

In every trial your goal is simply to press the m key if the square is green and the v key if the square is red.

At the end of the experiment a table will appear that shows your mean reaction time for congruent and incongruent trials. A congruent trial is when the location of the square matched the location of the finger that you used to make the response (e.g., a green square requires a left hand response, so a congruent trial is one where the green square is on the left). Likewise an incongruent trial is one where the location of square is opposite the location of the finger used to make the response (e.g., a green square on the right). The expected result is that your reaction time will be faster for congruent than for incongruent conditions.

Additional References

De Houwer, J., Crombez, G., Baeyen, F. & Hermans, D. (2001). On the generality of the affective Simon Effect. *Cognition and Emotion, 15* (2), 189-206.

Hommel, B. (1993). The role of attention for the Simon Effect. *Psychological Research/Psychologische Forschung 55,* 208-222.

Hommel, B. (1995). S-R compatibility and the Simon Effect: Toward an empirical clarification. *Journal of Experimental Psychology: Human Perception and Performance, 21,* 764-775.

Ivanoff, J., Klein, R. & Lupianez, J. (2002). Inhibition of return with the Simon Effect: An omnibus analysis and its implications. *Perception & Psychophysics, 64* (2), 318-327.

Kornblum, S., Hasbroucq, T. & Osman, A. (1990). Dimensional overlap: Cognitive basis for stimulus-response compatibility - A model and taxonomy. *Psychological Review,* 97, 253-270.

Miller, G.A., Galanter, E. & Pribram, K. (1960). *Plans and the Structure of Behavior.* New York: Holt, Rinehart, & Winston.

Basic Questions

1. Both the Stroop and the Simon Effect seem like similar cognitive processes because reaction times slow down due to interference. What is the major difference between these two phenomenon?

2. After completing this lab you notice that you answer the desk phone with a different hand depending on which side the receiver cord is hanging down from. For example, if the phone cord is on the right side, you answer it with your right hand. How can you explain this behavior?

3. After buying a new stove, you find that you are continuously turning on the wrong elements. On this new stove, the controls for the elements are on the left-hand side and look like the picture below. Although there are pictures of the element that each button corresponds with, you are still having problems. Why are you having problems and how could you redesign your stove to help you?

4. You regularly miss the turnoff for your favorite restaurant, although you've been going there for the last four years. Until now you've always thought your sense of direction was bad because you miss the turnoff. Although the restaurant is on the right hand side of the highway, the sign indicating the turnoff is on the left hand side (although it is a large sign). What do you suggest was your problem and how could the restaurant change the situation, so you don't miss the turnoff?

5. You've injured your arm in a skiing accident and now you have it in a cast. Your psychology professor does not have a great deal of sympathy for you, so she decides not to give you an extension on your major paper. You sit down to type out your essay, but it is awkward because you can only use one hand. If you injured your right arm, what word would take longer to type, "was" or "oil"? Explain your answer.

Advanced Questions

1. One of the car companies is introducing a new, wild-looking, futuristic car onto the market. It has a streamlined body, bucket seats and more buttons than you've ever seen in a car. It gets great gas mileage on the highway and in town. You notice that the rear bumper looks funny when you realize that the signal lights are positioned on the left-hand side of the bumper, just on the outside of the break lights. When they are activated, a large arrow flashes green for a left turn and red for a right turn. Although a large arrow is flashing and pointing in the direction of the turn, you still think they will be a problem. What kind of problems do you foresee?

2. Your little brother and his friend are playing a hand slapping game called, "Say Uncle". Person A holds their hands out in front of them, palms up while person B holds their hands directly over person A's, palms down. The person whose hands are on the bottom tries to slap the other person's hands as hard as possible in an attempt to get them to say "Uncle" or that they give up. Their opponent, however, has to try and remove their hands before getting hit. If the person evades a slap, they switch roles and they become the hitter. You notice that your brother is pretty fast slapping his friend's right hand with his right hand, but is slow (and usually misses) hitting his opponent's left hand with his right hand. What kind of advice should you give your brother?

3. As a way of decreasing bicycle/automobile collisions, the safety commissioner is trying to change the hand signals that cyclists give when they are turning. His logic is that the drivers can not see the hand signals in time, so they run into the bicycles. According to the Simon Effect, what would be a

good start to changing the hand signals? Remember the goal is to decrease the motorist's reaction time to the cyclists, so they don't run into them.

Discussion Questions

1. As a runner, you've noticed that when oncoming drivers first spot you running on the road, they tend to steer their car towards you, but then they correct themselves and go around you. Discuss why you think this is happening and how you can do something about it?

2. How could a company that makes heavy equipment and machinery benefit from knowing about this cognitive phenomenon?

5.1 THE MODAL MODEL

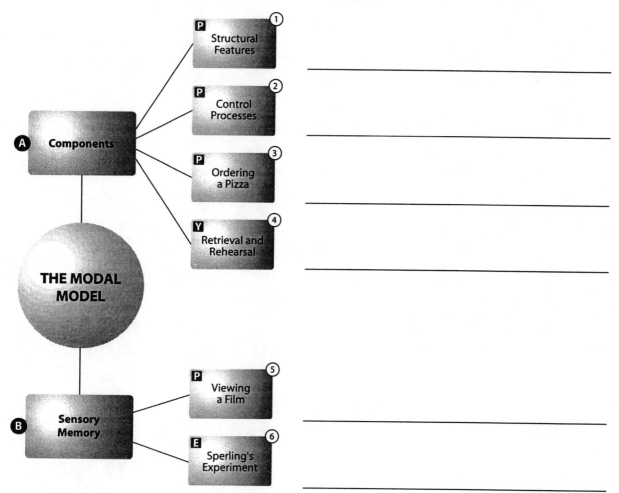

_____

_____

_____

_____

_____

_____

Ⓐ **What are the basic features of the modal model?**

① **Principle:** What are the three structural features of the modal model, and how long does each one hold information? (139)
② **Principle:** What are two control processes? (139)
③ **Principle:** Describe how the structural features and control processes interact during a task such as ordering a pizza, or pick another task that involves holding information in memory. (140)
④ **Your Experience:** Describe a situation in which you had trouble retrieving something from LTM (a memory was in there, but you couldn't get it out) and another situation in which rehearsal was needed to keep an item in memory.

Ⓑ **What is sensory memory?**

⑤ **Principle:** What is the function of sensory memory in the perception of film? (142)
⑥ **Experiment:** Describe the whole-report and partial-report procedures that were used to determine the duration of sensory memory. (Sperling; 143)

5.2 DISTINGUISHING BETWEEN STM & LTM I

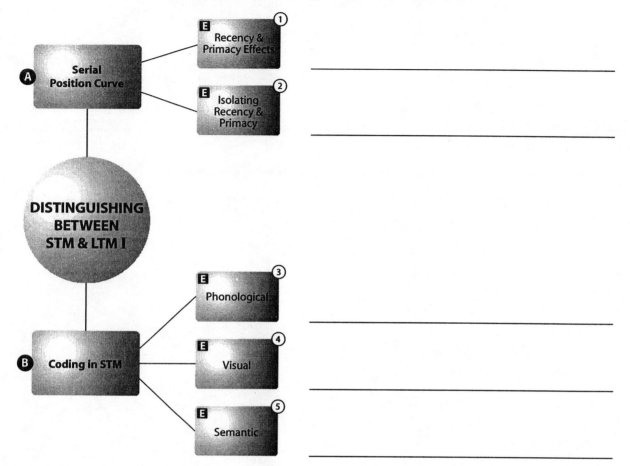

A **How is the serial position curve measured and what does it tell us?**

① **Principle:** Which part of the serial position curve indicates the recency effect? The primacy effect? (146)

② **Experiment:** How was the procedure for measuring the serial position curve modified to selectively affect the primacy effect? The recency effect? Which effect is associated with STM, and which is associated with LTM? (Glanzer & Cunitz; 147)

B **What is the distinction between physiological coding and mental coding, and between visual coding, phonological coding, and semantic coding?**

③ **Experiment:** How was phonological coding in STM demonstrated by analyzing errors in a letter-identification experiment? (Conrad; 150)

④ **Experiment:** How was visual coding in STM demonstrated by having participants identify Chinese radicals? How was phonological coding determined by having people identify Chinese characters? (Zhang & Simon; 150)

⑤ **Experiment:** How was semantic coding in STM demonstrated by the release from proactive interference effect? (Be sure you understand proactive interference and why it differed for the groups in this experiment.) (Wickens; 151)

5.3 DISTINGUISHING BETWEEN STM & LTM II

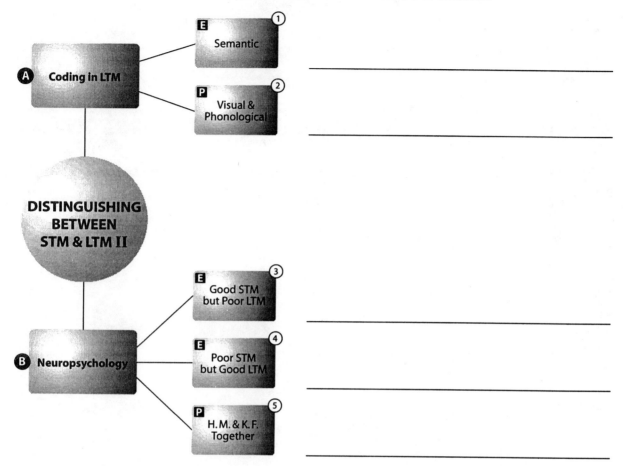

A **What is the predominant type of coding in LTM?**

① **Experiment:** How did the experiment that used a passage about Galileo and the telescope demonstrate the importance of semantic coding in LTM? (Sachs; 153)

② **Principle:** Give examples of visual and physiological codes in LTM. (153)

B **How do the memory problems of people with brain damage help distinguish between STM and LTM?**

③ **Experiment (Neuropsychology):** Describe the case of H.M. How were his STM and LTM affected by his brain damage? What kind of dissociation does this case demonstrate? (Scoville & Milner; 154)

④ **Experiment (Neuropsychology):** Describe the case of K.F. How were her STM and LTM affected? (Shallice & Warrington; 155)

⑤ **Principle:** What can we conclude about STM and LTM from the results of H.M. and K.F., taken together? (155)

5.4 PROPERTIES OF SHORT-TERM MEMORY

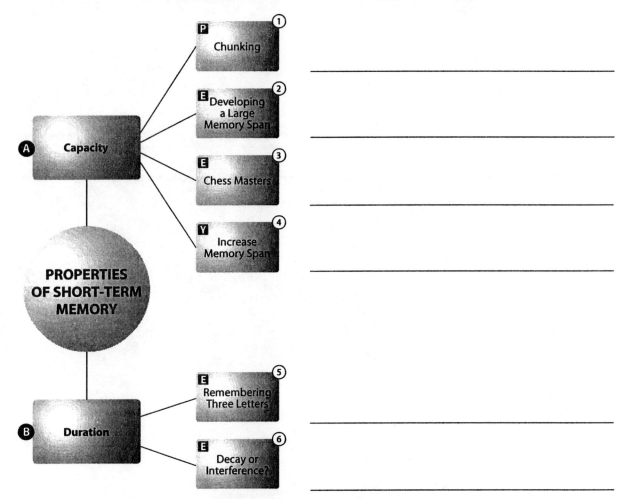

A **Why is it important to be able to hold small amounts of information for brief periods?**

① **Principle:** What is chunking? What is a chunk? (157)

② **Experiment:** How did the college student, S. F., use chunking to increase his digit span to 79? (Ericsson; 158)

③ **Experiment:** Describe the experiment that compared the memory of chess masters and beginning players. What can we conclude from the finding that the masters' performance was better in one condition, but not in the other condition? (Chase & Simon; 158)

④ **Your Experience:** Are there any situations in which you have used chunking to increase your memory span? Is there a way you can apply chunking to your studying for the next cognitive psychology exam?

B **How long does information remain in STM if rehearsal is prevented?**

⑤ **Experiment:** How long can a person remember three letters? What mechanism was first proposed to account for the decrease in memory with time? (Brown; Peterson & Peterson; 159)

⑥ **Experiment:** How were the results of the experiment in 5, above, reanalyzed? What did the reanalysis indicate about the mechanism responsible for the difficulty in remembering the letters? (Keppel & Underwood; 160)

5.5 WORKING MEMORY I

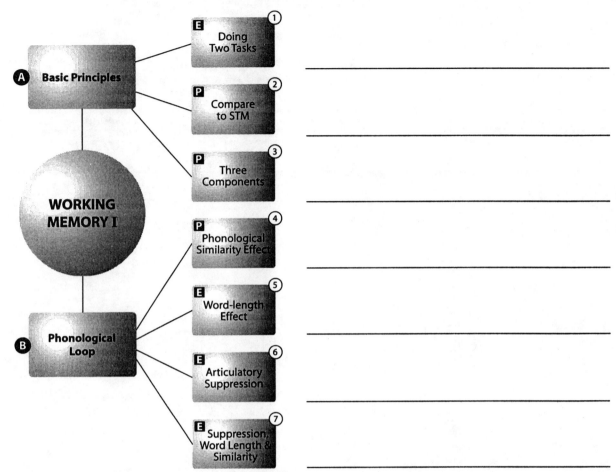

A **Why was working memory proposed and what are its basic components?**

① **Experiment:** Describe the experiment that showed that people can do two tasks at once. (Baddeley & Hitch; 161)

② **Principle:** Describe two ways working memory differs from STM? (162)

③ **Principle:** Describe the three components of working memory. (162)

B **How do various "effects" illustrate the properties of the phonological loop?**

④ **Principle:** What is the phonological similarity effect? How can it be demonstrated? (164)

⑤ **Experiment:** What is the word-length effect? How does memory compare for long and short words? Why do American children have greater digit spans than Welsh children? (Baddeley; 165)

⑥ **Experiment:** What is articulatory suppression? How is it achieved? Why does it interfere with memory? (Baddeley; 166)

⑦ **Experiment:** What does articulatory suppression do to the word length effect? To the phonological similarity effect for hearing words? For reading words? Why is there a difference? (Baddeley; 166)

5.6 WORKING MEMORY II

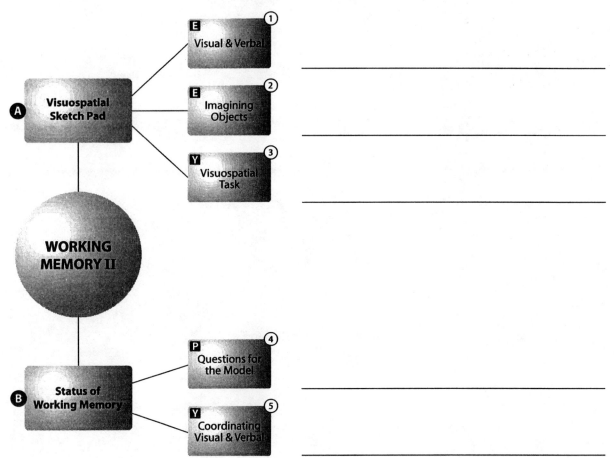

_____

_____

_____

_____

_____

(A) **How can various tasks demonstrate properties of the visuospatial sketch pad?**

(1) **Experiment:** How can the spatial and verbal tasks that involve imaging an "F" or indicating nouns in a sentence, which were described in Chapter 4 (See Map 4.3, Question 7), be explained in terms of working memory? (Brooks; 168)

(2) **Experiment:** How is the task of subtracting one picture from another affected by saying "la, la, la"? How is this result explained by the operation of working memory? (Brandimonte; 169)

(3) **Your Experience:** Describe an example from your own experience, when you have used your visuospatial sketch pad to accomplish a task.

(B) **Is the working memory model the "final word" on the short-term mechanism?**

(4) **Principle:** What are some things that the present working memory model has difficulty explaining? Why has there been little research on the central executive? (172)

(5) **Your Experience:** Think of a task or behavior from your experience that involves coordinating the action of your visuospatial sketch pad and phonological loop.

5.7 WORKING MEMORY & THE BRAIN

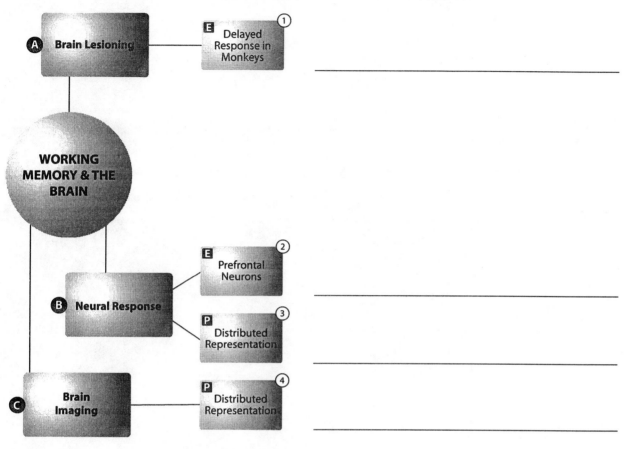

A What do the effects of brain damage on memory tell us about the physiology of working memory?

① **Experiment:** How does lesioning the prefrontal cortex affect a monkey's performance in the delayed response task? (Goldman-Rakic; 172)

B What does recording from single neurons tell us about the physiology of working memory?

② **Experiment:** Describe how some neurons in the prefrontal cortex respond during the delayed response task. (Funahashi; 173)

③ **Principle:** What does it mean to say that working memory is "distributed" in the brain? (174)

C What does brain imaging tell us about the physiology of working memory?

④ **Principle:** How does brain imaging research provide evidence that working memory involves distributed brain activity? (175)

Apparent Motion

If two stimuli are briefly flashed in rapid succession, observers will sometimes report seeing motion between the two stimuli. Reports of this type of apparent motion were investigated near the beginning of the 20th century by Gestalt psychologists (most notably Wertheimer). They noticed, among other things, that the timing of the flashes was important in determining whether or not motion was seen. If the time between the offset of the first stimulus and the onset of the second stimulus (called the interstimulus interval or ISI) is very short, observers simply see two dots presented nearly simultaneously. If the ISI is very long observers see one dot flash on and off and then the other flash on and off. For intermediate ISIs the first dot seems to turn off, move through the space between the dots and appear at the position of the second dot.

Korte (1915) noted that the ISI thresholds for seeing motion versus being too short varied with the spatial separation of the stimuli. The farther apart the stimuli were the longer the ISI needed to be for a good motion percept. These findings, and others, were formulated in a set of "Korte's laws" that have been used to describe aspects of apparent motion.

The relationship between spatial separation and ISI threshold is consistent with a variety of theories that hypothesize that the visual system builds a motion percept. For larger separations, the stimulus must "move" a farther distance, which presumably requires a greater length of time. This experiment allows you to see apparent motion in one of its simplest forms and to demonstrate Korte's law for yourself.

Apparent motion is the basis of movement in all television, movies, and computer animation. The screen actually shows a rapid succession of still images, the perceived motion is entirely "apparent" and illusory.

For registration information go to http://coglab.wadsworth.com.

A window will fill the entire screen. Press the space bar key to start a trial. After pressing the space bar, a small fixation square will appear in the middle of the screen. Fixate this square. It will disappear after one and a half seconds. Half a second later a dot will appear on the right, disappear, and then a dot will appear on the left and disappear. These stimuli will then cycle back and forth repeatedly. Each of the dots is presented for 150 milliseconds; the duration of the blank between dots (the ISI) is variable.

Your task is to adjust the ISI until the motion percept is as strong as you can make it. You can increase the ISI by 20 milliseconds by pressing the i key. You can decrease the ISI by 20 milliseconds by pressing the k key. The ISI can never become negative.

After you are satisfied that the motion percept is as strong as you can make it, press the space bar to start the next trial. The spacing of the dots will vary from trial to trial. There are five spacings and five replications for each spacing, for a total of 25 trials.

At the end of the experiment a graph will appear that plots the average Best ISI (in milliseconds) as a function of distance from the center of the screen (the number is the proportion of screen width). You should find that the best ISI increases with distance. This would confirm some aspects of Korte's laws of apparent motion.

Additional References

Kaneoke, Y., Bundou, M., Koyama, S., Suzuki, H., & Kakigi, R. (1997). Human cortical area responding to stimuli in apparent motion. *Neuroreport, 8*, 677-682.

Kersten, D., Mamassian, P., & Knill, D. C. (1997) Moving cast shadows induce apparent motion in depth. *Perception, 26*(2), 171-192.

Mather, G. (1988). Temporal properties of apparent motion in subjective figures. *Perception, 17*, 729-736.

Morgan, M. J. (1992). Spatial filtering precedes motion detection. *Nature, 355*, 344-346.

Muckli, L., Kriegeskorte, N., Lanfermann, H., Zanella, F. E., Singer, W., & Goebel, R. (2002). Apparent motion: Event-related functional magnetic resonance imaging of perceptual switches and states. *Journal of Neuroscience, 22*(9), RC 219 (1-5).

Peterhans, E., & von der Heydt, R. (1991). Subjective contours: Bridging the gap between psychophysics and physiology. *Trends in Neurosciences, 14*, 112-119.

Basic Questions

1. What is the interstimulus interval or ISI?

2. Would your results agree with Korte's Law if the graph showed the interstimulus interval going from 43ms to 87ms to 122ms to 135ms to 205ms as the distance between the presented dots increased? Why?

3. How does this lab help to explain why the flashing arrow looks like it is pointing to the entrance of the university café?

4. Why do we perceive movement when we are watching television?

Advanced Questions

1. You are sitting on a bus looking out the window at another bus beside yours. As the other bus pulls away, you get the feeling that you are moving backwards. Explain what is going on.

2. You are watching a new Science fiction alien movie. You notice that the aliens do not move around like humans so; they seem to jump from one place to another. How do you think the film editors could have made it seem like they jumped from one place to another very quickly?

Discussion Questions

1. Discuss the relationship between the interstimulus interval and the distance between the objects as it relates to what is perceived by the viewer.

2. Discuss how designers of cartoons use the parameters of the apparent motion phenomenon when designing their sketches. How much time do you think is needed for the production of a 30-minute segment? Do you think the time of creation has reduced dramatically with computer programs?

Partial Report

In the early beginnings of psychology, researchers were interested in something called the "perceptual span." This quest was to determine how much information could be gathered in a single percept. For example, when you read text, how many letters can you interpret in a single glance? Or, how many coins can you distinguish if you briefly glance at them? The goal was to identify the limits of perceptual abilities. A variety of ingenious studies seemed to draw similar conclusions that people could accurately report about 4.5 items from a brief percept. This fact was built into many theories of cognition until a set of experiments by George Sperling (1960) proved it wrong.

Sperling suggested that the 4.5 item limit was imposed not by the capabilities of the perceptual system, but by observers' abilities to recall items that had been seen. To test this possibility he designed a partial report experiment. This laboratory allows you to participate in a version of this experiment.

In Sperling's original experiment, the observer saw a three by three matrix of random letters on each trial. The letters were flashed for a very short period of time (50 milliseconds). After the letter matrix turned off, one of three tones sounded, and the observer reported the letters from the row associated with the tone. If the tone was presented directly after offset of the letters, Sperling found that observers were nearly 100% accurate in reporting letters from the indicated row.

This result destroys theories that hypothesized that percepts hold only 4 - 5 items. Because the tone was sounded after the letters disappeared, observers must be focusing on the appropriate row as it is stored in some type of sensory store of perceptual information. Moreover, since perfect performance is found regardless of which row is indicated, the sensory store must contain a nearly perfect representation of the total visual percept. Thus, perceptual span was not 4.5 items, but essentially every item in the visual field.

What determined perceptual span in the earlier experiments was not limits of the perceptual system, but the time needed to report the seen items. The duration of information in sensory store is very brief (a few hundred milliseconds), so as observers report what they see, items in sensory store fade away. By the time observers report on 4 or 5 items, the sensory store information is gone and recall is finished.

Sperling also found a way to measure the duration of information in sensory store. When he increased the time between the offset of the letter matrix and the onset of the tone cue, he found that recall of letters became worse. If the tone was delayed by a full second, recall was comparable to the 4.5 items found in other experiments.

When these experimental results were reported in 1960 they revolutionized both our understanding of perception and memory and the experimental methods with which cognitive psychology was studied. There have subsequently been thousands of studies on the sensory (also called iconic) store and it is a part of many theories of cognition.

For registration information go to http://coglab.wadsworth.com.

After clicking on the start button, a window will fill the entire screen. Press the space bar to start a trial; the screen will go dark and a small fixation square will appear in the middle of the screen. Fixate this square. It will disappear after one and a half seconds. Half a second letter a three by three matrix of letters will be flashed for 150 milliseconds. Some time after the offset of the letter matrix, an arrow (>) will indicate which row you are to report. Type the letters from the indicated row. Guess if you do not know what the letters were. You can make up to three guesses for every trial.

When you are ready, press the space bar for the next trial. There are a total of 60 trials, with the same basic task in every one. Simply report the letters that flashed from the indicated row. As you go through the experiment, keep your eyes steady on the fixation mark, then do not move them until after the matrix disappears. There is no method for discarding a trial in this experiment, so try to make certain you are ready as you start a trial.

At the end of the experiment a graph will appear that plots the percentage of letters correctly reported as a function of the delay between letter matrix offset and arrow indicator onset (in milliseconds). As the delay increases from 20 to 1000 milliseconds, you should find that the percentage correct drops.

The number of letters in your sensory store would be the total number of letters in the matrix (9) multiplied by the proportion (percentage divided by 100) of items you reported. For the 1000 millisecond (one second) delay, you may find that your proportion multiplied by 9 is about 4.5 items.

Additional References

Haber, R. N. (1983). The impending demise of the icon: A critique of the concept of iconic storage in visual information processing. *Behavioral and Brain Sciences, 6*, 1-54.

Kling, S. C., & Long, G. M. (1983). The effects of target size and retinal location on a partial report task of iconic memory. *Bulletin of the Psychonomic Society, 21*, 435-438.

Massaro, D. W. & Loftus, G. R. (1996). Sensory and perceptual storage: Data and theory. In E.L. Bjork and R.A. Bjork (Eds.), *Memory, Second Edition, Handbook of Perception and Cognition,* San Diego: Academic Press, 67-99.

Yeomans, J. M., & Irwin, D. E. (1985). Stimulus duration and partial report performance. *Perception and Psychophysics, 37*, 163-169.

Basic Questions

1. What does perceptual span refer to?

2. How was the earlier concept of perceptual span different from Sperling's idea?

3. What is the partial report method and how does it help one to understand sensory memory?

4. What is the difference between a partial-report technique and a whole-report technique for testing memory?

Advanced Questions

1. What should your results look like and why?

2. In the real world, does the idea of a sensory store "fading snapshot" parallel visual processing in a stable environment?

Discussion Questions

1. Discuss how this CogLab is similar to Metacontrast Masking.

2. Discuss why it may be adaptive to have a sensory store.

Serial Position

This demonstration explores effects of list position on free recall. In many instances we are presented with a list of items and must remember each of the items (e.g., grocery lists). If the order of the items is not required for accurate recall, the task is said to be unordered, or "free".

A general finding of free recall tasks is that recall of an item is strongly influenced by its position in a list. A common finding is that the last few items in the list are remembered best (called a recency effect), the first few items are remembered fairly well (called a primacy effect), but items in the middle of the list are not recalled very well at all. Surprisingly, this property holds for many types of items and for a wide variety of durations (seconds to years). The effect of serial position has played a major role in the development of memory theories.

For registration information go to http://coglab.wadsworth.com.

Start a trial by pressing the Next trial button. The empty space on the left of the window will show a sequence of ten letters, each presented for one second. After the full sequence has been presented, the buttons on the right will become clickable. Your task is to click on the buttons that correspond to the letters in the sequence just shown in any order. You cannot click on more than ten buttons, and each button can only be clicked once for a given sequence. After you have finished clicking on all the buttons, click on Next trial to start the next sequence. The experiment includes fifteen sequences, with different letters making up the sequence each time.

Feel free to use whatever mental tricks you find help you recall the consonants. Some people mentally (or verbally) rehearse items to themselves. Some people also click on the buttons for the last few items in the list before they fade from memory.

You can also create variations of this experiment by changing what you do during presentation of the sequence, or how you report back items. For example, if you try to recall the letters in the sequence in the order they were presented, you will likely find that the recency effect disappears. If you repeat a phrase to yourself during presentation of the sequence, you will likely find that your overall performance drops.

When the experiment finishes, a new window will appear that plots the percentage of times you correctly recalled an item at each position in the sequence. You should find that you tend to have higher percentages correct for the first (serial position 1) and last (serial position 10) items in the list. For the middle positions (around serial position 5), you may find that your percentage correct is much lower.

Additional References

Brodsky, M., McNeil, M., Doyle, P., Fossett, T. R., Timm, N.H. & Park, G.H. (2003). Auditory serial position effects in story retelling for non-brained-injured participants and persons with aphasia. *Journal of Speech, Language, and Hearing Research, 46*(5), 1124-1132.

Howard, M. W. & Kahana, M. J. (1999). Contextual variability and serial position effects in free recall. *Journal of Experimental Psychology: Learning, Memory, and Cognition, 25,* 923-941.

Pieters, R. G. & Bijmolt, T. H. (1997). Consumer memory for television advertising: A field study of duration, serial position, and competition effects. *Journal of Consumer Research, 23*(4), 362-372.

Stefanova, E. D., Kostic, V., Ziropadja, L., Markovic, M. & Ocic, G. (2002). Serial position learning effects in patients with aneurysms of the anterior communicating artery. *Journal of Clinical and Experimental Neuropsychology, 24*(5), 687-694.

Basic Questions

1. In a free-recall memory task, if your recall is impaired at the beginning of the list of items, it is called _____, while impairment on the items near the end of the list it is called _____.

2. What would the graph have to look like if your results supported the serial position effect hypotheses?

3. What do you think would happen to the graph of the results of this CogLab if you were asked to do a few seconds of mental arithmetic tasks before you were allowed to recall the letters?

4. When your roommate is in the shower, he has the annoying habit of loudly singing the song that wakes him up in the morning. The unfortunate thing about his singing is that he can only remember the last part of the song. How can this CogLab explain his odd behavior?

Advanced Questions

1. Some theorists have suggested that the recency and the primacy effects in this demonstration is due to the operation of separate kinds of memory—long term and short term. Based on your experience with this demonstration, which effect probably comes from long term memory and which comes from short term memory?

2. As a waiter, you realize that your tips are highly correlated with delivering the right drinks to the right customer. One night after a big concert, you have a large table come in for late night drinks. As you go around the table, you remember the first four and the last three, but you have the write down the middle three drink orders. How can this lab explain your behavior?

Discussion Questions

1. Discuss how the results of the serial position CogLab could help a student study for a comprehensive final exam.

2. Discuss how the serial position task effect could be used to assess memory deficits in certain populations. Think about the populations that may show abnormal serial position effects.

Memory Span

Many theories of cognition propose that there is a short-term or working memory system that is able to hold a limited amount of information for a short period of time. The memory span experiment is one measure of working memory capacity. In this experiment participants are given a list of items and asked to recall the list. The list length is varied to see at what list length participants will make few errors. That list length is the memory span for that subject on that task. Individuals with larger memory spans can better keep in mind different stimuli, and this seems to give them an advantage for a wide variety of cognitive tasks. Memory span has been linked to performance on intelligence tests, standardized tests, reading skills, problem solving and a variety of other cognitive tasks.

The very existence of short-term memory is largely based on memory span types of experiments, as it was noted that memory span was approximately seven (plus or minus two) for a wide variety of stimuli. This suggested a simple storage system that held approximately seven items. Later studies demonstrated that memory span could be systematically influenced by a variety of stimulus characteristics. For example, when the stimuli are letters that sound alike (e.g., d, b, p, t) memory span is shorter. Likewise, memory span is shorter for lists of long words (e.g., encyclopedia, refrigerator) than for lists of short words (e.g., book, stove). These findings have suggested that capacity of short-term memory is controlled by verbal processes. This experiment allows you to measure your memory span for a variety of stimulus types.

For registration information go to http://coglab.wadsworth.com.

Start a trial by pressing the Next Trial button. On the left of the window will appear a sequence of items, with each item presented for one second. After the full sequence has been presented, the buttons on the right will show labels for item names, including those just shown. Your task is to click on the buttons just shown in the same order that the items were presented. After you have finished clicking on all the buttons to recreate the list, click on Next Trial to start the next sequence.

The experiment includes five types of stimuli: Numbers, Letters that sound different, Letters that sound the same, Short words, and Long words. In each case your task is simply to report the items you saw, in the order they were presented. Each stimulus type will be presented five times, with varying list lengths.

List length is varied, for each type of stimuli, to find the longest list for which you can correctly recreate the sequence. Being correct means that you both recall all the items in the sequence and click on the buttons in the same order the items appeared in the sequence. Any mistake (recalling too many items, recalling too few items, or recalling items in the wrong order) counts as Incorrect. There is no way to correct mistakes in button presses, so be careful in your selections. After clicking on Next Trial, you will be given feedback on your response to the previous sequence (Correct/Incorrect) before the next sequence is presented.

If you are correct for a given sequence, then the next sequence for that stimulus type will be one item longer. If you are incorrect, the next sequence for that stimulus type will be one item shorter. In this way, the length of the sequence converges on the longest list length that you can reliably report back.

When the experiment finishes, a new window will appear that gives the length of the last sequence for each stimulus type. This is an estimate of your memory span.

The literature on memory span suggests that the memory span for Numbers, Letters that sound different, and Short words should be around seven items. Memory span for Letters that sound the same and Long words should be shorter. There are five trials for each stimulus type. The maximum memory span measurable with this experiment is ten, so if you were correct on the last trial for a stimulus type and your list length was ten; your memory span may actually be greater. This would indicate that you have an excellent short-term memory.

Additional References

Conant, L. L., Fastenau, P. S., Giordani, B., Boivin, M. J., Opel, B. & Nseyila, D. D. (1999). Modality specificity of memory span tasks among Zaïrian children: A developmental perspective. *Journal of Clinical and Experimental Neuropsychology, 21*(3), 375-384.

Cowan, N., Saults, J. S., Winterowd, C. & Sherk, M. (1991). Enhancement of 4-year-old children's memory span for phonologically similar and dissimilar word lists. *Journal of Experimental Psychology, 51*(1), 30-52.

Hitch, G.J., Towse, J.N., & Hutton, U. (2001). What limits children's working memory span? Theoretical accounts and applications for scholastic development. *Journal of Experimental Psychology: General, 130*(2), 184-198.

May, C. P., Hasher, L. & Kane, M. J. (1999). The role of interference in memory span. *Memory & Cognition, 27,* 759-767.

Basic Questions

1. What cognitive ability does memory span measure? On average, how large is the memory span?

2. If the results of the lab indicated that you had a large memory span, what might this suggest about your ability to keep and work with information in your memory store?

3. Memory span ability has been linked to performance on what specific cognitive tasks?

4. How could you redesign the lab to increase an individual's memory span?

Advanced Questions

1. How are memory span and operation span similar?

2. Explain how memory span might be based on "verbal processes".

Discussion Questions

1. Discuss how having a good working memory ability might be related to improved cognitive performance.

2. Discuss how some researchers explain the differences between short-term memory and working memory.

Brown-Peterson

In the 1940's memory loss was widely considered to be the result of new information interfering with previously learned information. In the late 1950's two groups of researchers (one named Brown and a husband and wife team named Peterson) published data that forced a new interpretation of human memory.

In the memory task, the participant viewed a trigram of consonants (e.g., GKT, WCH,...) and then performed a number of algebraic computations (e.g., counting backwards by 3's) for less than 20 seconds. The data showed that recall of the trigram was less likely as the participant worked on the algebraic computations for longer durations.

Solving math problems seems to be very different from recalling consonant trigrams, so it was unlikely that there was any interference to disturb the memory of the trigram. The conclusion was that there exists a short-term memory (STM) system that holds information for several seconds. Without an active effort by the participant, information in STM fades away (but see Keppel & Underwood, 1962, for an alternate explanation). Performing the distractor task prevented the participant from actively rehearsing the trigram. STM is now a fundamental part of most theories of cognitive psychology.

For registration information go to http://coglab.wadsworth.com.

A few seconds after clicking on the start button, a window will appear with a blank screen on the left and buttons on the right. Start the experiment by clicking on the Next Trial button.

On the left screen a trigram of letters will appear for two seconds. You will then be given a series of digits and asked to classify them as odd (press the o key) or even (press the e key). The duration of time spent classifying digits as odd or even will vary from one to twenty-one seconds. After correct completion of the classification task you will be prompted to recall the consonant trigram. From the buttons, select the consonants, in the correct order, that appeared before the classification task. After you have entered your guess, and are ready for the next trial, click on Next Trial button again.

For the trial to count, you must have correctly classified all the digits as odd or even. If your classification is incorrect, the trial will be repeated later in the experiment. Thus, to finish the experiment you must apply yourself to the digit classification task. There are a total of 30 trials that must be run to finish the experiment.

At the end of the experiment a graph will appear that plots the percentage of correctly recalled trigrams as a function of the duration of the distractor task (digit classification). For this calculation, a recall is correct only if it includes all the trigram letters in their correct order. You should find that the percentage correct decreases as distractor duration increases.

Additional References

Bherer, L., Belleville, S. & Peretz, I. (2001). Education, age, and the Brown-Peterson technique. *Developmental Neuropsychology, 19,* 237-251.

Fleming, K., Goldberg, T. E., Gold, J. M. & Weinberger, D. R. (1995). Verbal working memory dysfunction in schizophrenia: use of a Brown-Peterson paradigm. *Psychiatry Research, 56*(2), 155-61.

Floden, D., Stuss, D. & Craik, F. (2000). Age differences in performances on two versions of the Brown-Peterson task. *Aging, Neuropsychology, and Cognition, 7*(4), 245-259.

Greene, R. (1996). The influence of experimental design: The example of the Brown-Peterson paradigm. *Canadian Journal of Experimental Psychology, 50*(2), 240-242.

Talasli, U. (1989). Proactive inhibition after self-paced study: An analysis of encoding in the Brown-Peterson paradigm. *Journal of General Psychology, 116*(3), 229-246.

Tehan, G., Hendry, L. & Kocinshki, D. (2001). Word length and phonological similarity effects in simple, complex, and delayed recall tasks: Implications for working memory. *Memory, 9*(4-6), 333-348.

Basic Questions

1. Why were participants asked to perform the task of determining whether a number was odd or even after the trigrams were presented?

2. What should have happened to your performance when the duration between the presentation of the trigram and the memory task increased?

3. What kind of memory task was this an example of, recall or recognition? What is the difference between the two types of memory tasks?

4. How does information get from short-term memory to long-term memory?

5. Immediately after your Psychology professor tells the class what chapters are on the midterm, your friend starts to give you his new cell phone number. When you find your pen to write your friend's new number down, you realize that you can't remember what chapters your professor said were on the midterm. What happened to the information about the test chapters?

Advanced Questions

1. What is the difference between primary and secondary memory?

2. How could the results of this Brown-Peterson task support the decay theory of forgetting?

Discussion Questions

1. Discuss the difference between the interference and decay theory of forgetting.

2. Discuss how encoding, storage, and retrieval are related to the Brown-Peterson CogLab.

Phonological Similarity

When people are asked to recall a list of items, their performance is usually worse when the items sound similar than when the items sound different (Conrad, 1964). Although this effect has become known as the phonological similarity effect, a better term is the acoustic similarity effect because what matters is that the items sound similar to each other.

What is most surprising about the phonological similarity effect is that it occurs even when there is no auditory input, such as when you read the items silently to yourself. This result has been taken as suggesting that people recode the information. If you used only a visual representation, you would be more likely to confuse items that looked similar (e.g., E and F). This idea is central to Baddeley's (1986) conception of the phonological loop, one of the components of working memory.

The phonological loop has two parts: the phonological store and the articulatory control process. The phonological store is a memory store that can retain speech-based (phonological) information for a short period of time. Unless rehearsed, the traces within the store are assumed to fade and decay within about 2 seconds, after which they are no longer usable. The second component is the articulatory control process, which is responsible for two different functions: it translates visual information into a speech-based code and deposits it in the phonological store; and it refreshes a trace in the phonological store, offsetting the decay process.

According to the phonological loop model, the reason that you get a phonological similarity effect when there is no auditory input is that the articulatory control process has converted the visual information into a phonological form. One key prediction is that if you somehow prevent the articulatory control process from converting the information, then the phonological similarity effect will be removed: in other words, recall of similar sounding and dissimilar sounding items will be equivalent. One way of preventing this recoding is to keep the articulatory control process busy doing something else.

This demo is based on an experiment reported by Murray (1968) and uses a technique called articulatory suppression to prevent the articulatory control process from recoding the visual information into phonological information. On half of the trials, you will see similar sound letters and on the other half of the trials you will see dissimilar sounding letters. On some trials, you will be asked to say "One, two, three, four, one, two, three, four, ..." out loud over and over. You should start speaking when told to start, and you should continue until you see the response buttons become active.

For registration information go to http://coglab.wadsworth.com.

Start a trial by clicking once on the *Next Trial* button. On the left of the window will appear a sequence of letters, with each letter presented for one second. After the full sequence has been presented, the buttons on the right will show labels for the letters, including those just shown. Your task is to click on the buttons just shown *in the same order* that the letters were presented. After you have finished clicking on all the buttons to recreate the list, click on *Next Trial* to start the next sequence.

On some trials, you will see the instruction "Speak" appear before the letters. You should repeatedly say "One, Two, Three, Four, One, Two, Three, Four, ..." out loud until you see the response buttons become active. You do not need to speak loudly, but you should try to speak quickly. You should avoid doing this lab in a public space so that you do not disturb other people around you. If you see the word "Quiet" do not say anything out loud.

Being correct means that you both recall all the items in the sequence and click on the buttons in the same order the items appeared in the sequence. Any mistake (recalling too many items, recalling too few items, or recalling items in the wrong order) counts as Incorrect. There is no way to correct mistakes in button presses, so be careful in your selections.

The experiment includes 32 trials. Half involve articulatory suppression, and half do not. Half have letters that sound similar to each other and half have letters that all sound different.

When the experiment finishes, a new window will appear that gives the proportion of dissimilar-sounding items you recalled and the proportion of similar-sounding items you recalled. You should do worse when the items sound similar.

Additional References

Coltheart, V. (1993). Effects of phonological similarity and concurrent irrelevant articulation on short-term-memory recall of repeated and novel word lists. *Memory & Cognition, 21,* 539-545.

Copeland, D. & Radvansky, G. (2001). Phonological similarity in working memory. *Memory & Cognition,* 774.

Larsen, J. D., Baddeley, A. & Andrade, J. (2000). Phonological similarity and the irrelevant speech effect: Implications for models of short-term verbal memory. *Memory, 8*(3), 145-157.

Rogers, M. A. & Storkel, H. L. (1998). Reprogramming phonologically similar utterances: The role of phonetic features in pre-motor encoding. *Journal of Speech, Language, and Hearing Research, 41,* 258-274.

Basic Questions

1. What are the two parts of the phonological loop called?

2. What is the role of the phonological store?

3. How would your memory recall for the letters compare if a Phonological Similarity effect were found?

4. How is the articulatory control process affected by the articulatory suppression task?

1. Why is the articulatory suppression technique used in this CogLab?

2. The Phonological Similarity effect supports the idea of the phonological loop within the working memory. What other CogLabs or other cognitive concepts might also support the phonological loop?

Discussion Questions

1. Discuss the relationship between phonological similarity and memory span.

2. Discuss how phonological similarity could be used to look for working memory deficits or problems in a person or group of people.

Irrelevant Speech Effect

When people are asked to recall a list of items, their performance is usually worse when presentation of the list is accompanied by irrelevant speech. The speech does not need to be in a language that the subject knows, and doesn't even have to be real speech. Nonsense speech (such as "ba da ga") works just as well. One reason that this phenomenon, known as the irrelevant speech effect, has attracted a lot of attention is because it seems strange that auditory information (the irrelevant speech stimuli) would interfere with visual information (the items you are trying to remember).

Although there is still no generally agreed upon explanation for this effect, there are at least three different explanations (Neath, 2000). One theory attributes the disruption to interference in working memory. The visual items are translated into a phonological code which is stored in the same part of memory (the phonological store) as the irrelevant speech. Another attributes the effect to a disruption of order information. You remember the items, but it is information about the order that is lost. A third attributes the effect to a combination of two factors, an attentional component and an interference component.

For registration information go to http://coglab.wadsworth.com.

This lab requires a computer that can play sound. Before you start, please make sure that the volume of your computer/speakers is set to a comfortable level.

Start a trial by clicking once on the 'Next Trial' button. You will see 7 letters displayed one at a time. On half the trials, you will hear someone speaking in German; ignore this. The order of the conditions is random. After the list has been presented, the response buttons will become active. Your task is to click on the buttons in the same order that the letters were shown. After you have finished clicking on all the buttons to recreate the list, click on 'Next Trial' to start the next sequence.

Being correct means that you both recall all the items in the sequence and click on the buttons in the same order the items appeared in the sequence. Any mistake (recalling too many items, recalling too few items, or recalling items in the wrong order) counts as Incorrect. There is no way to correct mistakes in button presses, so be careful in your selections.

When the experiment finishes, a new window will appear that gives the proportion of items you recalled in the quiet condition and the proportion of items you recalled in the irrelevant speech condition. You should do worse when there is irrelevant speech.

Additional References

Ellermeier, W. & Hellbrück, J. (1998). Is level irrelevant in "irrelevant speech"? Effects of loudness, signal-to-noise ratio and binaural unmasking. *Journal of Experimental Psychology: Human Perception and Performance, 24*, 1406-1414.

Macken, W.J., Mosdell, N., & Jones, D.M. (1999). Explaining the irrelevant sound effect: Temporal distinctiveness or changing state? *Journal of Experimental Psychology: Learning, Memory and Cognition, 25*, 810-814.

Basic Questions

1. How could you change the methodology of this lab to study what specific kind of stimuli produce greater memory interference effects - irrelevant noise or irrelevant speech?

2. If you found that irrelevant speech interfered with your memory for visually presented material over irrelevant noise, what might this suggest to you about the kind of background music you could listen to while studying?

3. You are trying to study in the library, but there are people beside you who are whispering and talking. Could this situation be affecting your studying performance? Why or why not?

4. You are trying to watch an intense psychological thriller on television and you need to follow the character's actions very closely to understand what is going on. Your roommate, however, is walking around the apartment muttering into his cell phone. How is he affecting your ability to follow the characters in the movie?

5. If you were studying for your final exam in Biology and you haven't been doing well in the term and you need an "A" to pass this course, how could this lab help to structure your studying environment?

Advanced Questions

1. One theory that is used to explain the results of this lab is that there may be a disruption of the order of the to-be-remembered information. How could you add or re-examine the dependent measures of this lab so that you could address this theory?

2. You are trying to find your way to a friend's house for a party. You've been there once before but that was a long time ago. As you find yourself getting lost and driving in circles, you immediately turn your music down. After doing this lab, explain why this might make sense.

3. You work in a call center for an international company on the weekends for extra money. Everyone sits in a large warehouse behind small cubicles while dealing with customers on the phone. What kind of problems could you have in this kind of work environment that takes the irrelevant speech effect into consideration?

Discussion Questions

1. Discuss others areas in society, besides school, where you might find examples of the irrelevant speech effect. Be specific about the place and possible problems this effect might cause

2. From a methodological standpoint, there may be other factors that affect the degree of memory loss in the irrelevant speech effect. Some factors may include things like loudness of speech (reference provided), gender of speech, different languages or the number of different stimuli presented (more than one speech at the same time). Hypothesize how these and other factors you can think of may influence the overall effect. You can refer to the specific parts of the working memory; phonological loop; visuospatial pad and the executive control or other knowledge you have about memory, when formulating your hypotheses.

Modality Effect

People often have to recall a series of items in order, such as when recalling a phone number. When the list of items is heard (as opposed to read silently), people usually are very good at remembering the final list item. This advantage in recalling just the last one or two items when the list is heard is called the modality effect.

Modality effects can be seen with presentation modalities other than auditory (hearing). Lists that are lip-read or silently mouthed also produce an advantage for the last one or two items compared to silent visual presentation.

These effects had an enormous influence on the development of sensory memory. This memory system is supposed to store raw, unanalyzed sensory input. It can be thought of as a back-up system: if the information in this store is useful, recall can be enhanced.

The best explanation is that auditory presentation leads to an additional type of information compared to visual (Neath & Surprenant, 2003). When trying to recall the last item in the list, you are more likely to be successful if you also have some information about how the list sounds.

For registration information go to http://coglab.wadsworth.com.

Before the demonstration begins, make sure the volume on your computer/speakers is set at a comfortable level. If you are running this lab in a public space, please use headphones so that you do not disturb other people.

After clicking on the start button, a window will fill the entire screen. Start a trial by clicking once on the 'Next Trial' button. On half the trials, you will hear the digits 1-8 spoken in random order. On the other half of the trials, you will see the digits 1-8 appear. After the list has been presented, the response buttons will become active. Your task is to click on the buttons in the same order that the numbers were presented. After you have finished clicking on all the buttons to recreate the list, click on 'Next Trial' to start the next sequence.

Being correct means that you click on the buttons in the same order the items appeared in the sequence. There is no way to change your response once you've clicked on a button.

There are 30 trials, 15 visual and 15 auditory trials randomly intermixed. When the experiment finishes, a new window will appear that gives the proportion of items you recalled at each list position in the visual condition and in the auditory condition. You should do very well recalling the first item in both conditions. However, you should be much more accurate in recalling the last item when it was heard compared to when it was seen.

Additional References

Neath, I., & Surprenant, A. M. (2003). *Human Memory: An Introduction to Research, Data, and Theory* (Second Edition). Thomson Wadsworth: Belmont, CA.

Surprenant, A. M., Neath, I., & LeCompte, D. C. (1999). Irrelevant speech, phonological similarity, and presentation modality. *Memory, 7,* 405-420.

Basic Questions

1. Of the eight letters presented in the experiment, which letters had the lowest rate of recall? Which letter had the best rate of recall?

2. Which mode of list presentation had the higher rate of percentage recalled for the end items?

3. If you were making out your appointments for the day that you have to remember, why would it make more sense to say them out loud to yourself after writing them out, rather than just righting them down in your daily planner?

4. You are trying to decide whether or not to buy the CD that accompanies one of your textbooks. The CD is expensive, but it has a number of interactive activities and an auditory glossary. You are struggling in this class and you are concerned about your grades. If money is not an issue, should you purchase the CD or not?

5. You are following along with your favorite cooking show and trying to make fudge cake. They don't have time to go through the icing so they flash the ingredients on the screen during a break. Your icing doesn't taste right and you think that you forgot an item. If the recipe was visually presented on the screen, would it make sense that you forgot the last item in the recipe?

Advanced Questions

1. You have been hired to design a fresh new commercial for your University. Your goal is to have people remember the name of the University after the commercial is over. How could you use the modality effect to your advantage in making your commercial?

2. You are responsible for advertising the last class bash for your organization and you want to make it the largest one ever. You can either advertise in the campus newspaper or on the campus radio station. You choose to advertise with the radio station because the listening audience is greater. How can you use the modality effect to help design your catchy announcement so people remember to come to the party? Remember the mode of presentation.

Discussion Questions

1. Discuss how the modality effect is related to the idea of *Cognitive load*. According to this idea, learning will be impaired if the material causes a cognitive overload. Since the working memory is very limited, how would varying the modality reduce the cognitive load?

2. How could the results of this lab help you with improve your performance on tests as well as your overall academic performance?

Operation Span

Recent conceptions of memory have suggested that memory consists of a flexible workspace that not only stores information but also plays an active role in processing and manipulating information. This active process, however, seems to have a limited amount of resources to work with. One question that has been posed is whether the capacity is specific to verbal tasks or whether there is a general pool of resources that is used in every working memory task. Most previous researchers have used only verbal materials in measuring working memory capacity.

To determine whether there is a general capacity for all working memory tasks Turner and Engle (1989) developed a task called "operation-word-span" (OSPAN). In this task subjects are asked to read and verify a simple math problem (such as (4/2)-1=1) and then read a word after the operation (such as SNOW). After a series of problems and words had been presented, the subjects recall the words that followed each operation. The number of operation-word strings in a sequence is increased and decreased to measure the subject's operation span. Operation span measures predict verbal abilities and reading comprehension even though the subjects are solving mathematical problems. Engle and his colleagues have argued that this implicates a general pool of resources that is used in every type of working memory situation.

This demonstration allows you to measure your operation span using the procedure of Conway & Engle (1996).

For registration information go to http://coglab.wadsworth.com.

Start a trial by pressing the Next Trial button. Each trial has several parts. Start a trial by clicking once on the 'Next Trial' button. You will see a math problem of the form:

Is 10/2 + 2 = 7 ?

Read the math problem out loud and then answer the question. In this example, you would click once on the 'Yes' button because 10 divided by 2, plus 2 does equal 7.

You will then see a word. Read the word out loud. You will then see another math problem. At some point, you will be asked to recall all the words from the series. Click on the buttons that are labeled with words you have just seen in the order in which you saw the words. Your responses will be counted as correct only if you recall the words in the correct order.

Your operation span score is valid only if you were more than 85% accurate in evaluating the math problems. If you were more than 85% accurate in evaluating the math problems, you will see your operation span score at the end of the demonstration.

This score is the sum of the sequence lengths you recalled correctly. Thus, if you recalled the list of 2 words correctly, you would add 2 to your operation span score. If you recalled the list of 6 items correctly, you would add 6 to your operation span.

The first three trials were all of length 2, and were considered practice trials. Performance on these trials does not affect your accuracy score or you operation span score.

The literature on working memory capacity suggests that operation span correlates well with performance on other tasks, including ones involving memory and attention.

Additional References

Conway, A. & Engle, R. (1996). Individual differences in working memory capacity: More evidence for a general capacity theory. *Memory, 4*, 577-590.

Hitch, G., Towse, J. & Hutton, U. (2001). What limits children's working memory span? Theoretical accounts and applications for scholastic development. *Journal of Experimental Psychology: General, 130*, 184-198.

Basic Questions

1. Why do you think that your Operation Span would only be valid if it were 85% or higher on the math problems?

2. Why did the math problems and the words have to be read out loud instead of being done silently?

3. You are talking to some fellow classmates at a party in your residence. The friend you are talking to points to another group of people looking at you and laughing and you are curious what they are laughing about. When you go over to the group of people you see your best friend in the middle and she says that she was telling that group about a funny story that involved you but you didn't turn around when she yelled your name. What can be inferred about your ability to block out distractions and your Operation Span?

4. You are amazed by your boyfriend who can sit in front of the television set during Super bowl and never hear a word you have said for 2 hours, while you can complete conversations on the telephone using both lines, read the newspaper, do your nails, bake cookies and think about a math problem from class that day. In terms of controlling attention, how do the two of you compare?

5. Your father is teaching you to drive but you are having trouble remembering everything that you have to do to keep safe while on the road. Your father suggests that you say everything that you are doing out loud, so it will help you focus as you are performing the task. How is that comparable to this lab?

Advanced Questions

1. Although the Operation Span lab is found under the subcategory of memory, how is attention related to this phenomenon?

2. After doing this lab you discover that you have a relatively high OSPAN compared to your classmates. How might this affect your studying habits?

3. How could the three specific areas of working memory (phonological loop, visuospatial sketchpad and the executive control system) work together to perform this lab?

Discussion Questions

1. People with higher Operation Spans are said to be better at controlling their attention and are less affected by distractions. Discuss some situations where this may not be a good thing?

2. The concept of one's Operation Span has been correlated to reading ability and verbal comprehension. Why does this seem like a logical relationship?

Position Error

Many tasks require people to remember not only a set of items but also the order of the items. For example, a telephone number is meaningful only if the items are recalled in the correct order. When people do not recall an item in its correct order, the errors they make are systematic.

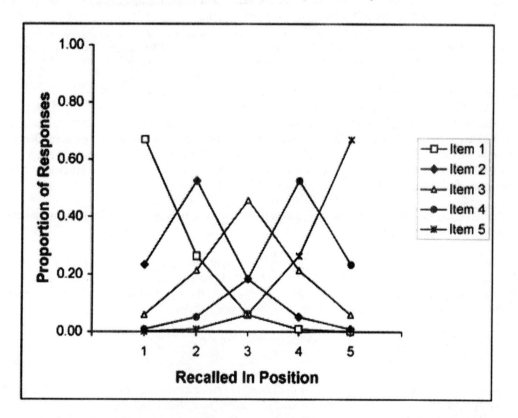

The graph above shows what these systematic errors would look like when people try to recall a five-item list in order. Most of the time, the items are recalled in the correct position. So, the line marked "Item 1" has its largest value at position 1; the line marked "Item 2" has its largest value at position 2; and so on. When an order error is made, the graph shows that the item is most likely to be recalled either 1 position too soon or 1 position too late. So, when Item 3 is not recalled in position 3, it is most likely to be recalled in position 2 or position 4.

Results like these have important implications for theories of memory. If all you look at is percent correct, then you might think that forgetting means that the information is lost from the memory system.

113

However, you are still remembering something about the item: you usually recall the item in a position adjacent to the correct position.

For registration information go to http://coglab.wadsworth.com.

Start a trial by clicking once on the 'Next Trial' button. You will see 7 letters displayed one at a time. After the list has been presented, the response buttons will become active. Your task is to click on the buttons in the same order that the letters were shown. After you have finished clicking on all the buttons to recreate the list, click on 'Next Trial' to start the next sequence.

Being correct means that you click on the buttons in the same order the items appeared in the sequence. There is no way to change your responses.

What follows are more detailed instructions.

Start a trial by clicking on the Next Trial button. On the left of the window will appear a sequence of 7 letters, with each letter presented for one second. After the full sequence has been presented, the buttons on the right will show labels for items just shown. Your task is to click on the buttons in the same order that the letters were presented. If you think the first letter was M, click on the button labeled M first. If you think the sixth letter was F, click on the button labeled F sixth.

After you have finished clicking on all the buttons to recreate the list, click on Next Trial to start the next sequence. There are 20 trials.

When the experiment finishes, a new window will appear that tells you the proportion of times you recalled each item in each position. You should find that your data look similar to the data shown in the graph: You should be most likely to recall an item in its original serial position, but when you made an error, the item should be most likely to be in an adjacent position.

Additional References

Estes, W. K. (1972). An associative basis for coding and organization in memory. In A. W. Melton & E. Martin (Eds.), *Coding processes in human memory.* Washington, DC: Winston.

Lee, C. L. & Estes, W. K. (1981). Item and order information in short-term memory: Evidence for multilevel perturbation processes. *Journal of Experimental Psychology: Human Learning and Memory, 7,* 149-169.

Basic Questions

1. When trying to recall the seven letters in order, which letter position should have shown the lowest rate of correct responses?

2   If the series of letters to be recalled were, MXFGKLC, which letter(s) would have the greatest probability of mistaking in the letter K's position?

3.   You are trying to remember the phone number, (705) 647-5893, but you do not have a pen to write it down. When you try to dial it, you make a mistake and dial, (705) 647-8593. Why does this misdial seem more possible than mixing up the 3 and the 8? What does this say about the errors that we make, are they random or systematic?

4.   You excitedly check your grade online to see how well your extensive studying worked for your cognitive exam. Your excitement fades fast when you see a failing grade for that test and you immediately find your professor. After checking, she notices that she has mixed up your grade with another student's grade when copying them to the online grade sheets. After doing this lab, explain how she could have mixed up the grades?

5.   You are trying out for the cheerleader squad at your school, but you are having trouble with the routine. The cheer goes; step, turn, kick, touch, leap, jump, splits, but you are leaping then touching. How can your error be explained through the position error gradient?

Advanced Questions

1.   What does the position error experiment tell us about our short- term memory system that the serial position effect does not expand on?

2.   Before doing this lab, you have always wondered why the Biology Lab Teaching Assistant is always calling you David, when your name is Sean. Why did this experiment explain this error to you?

Discussion Questions

1.   Discuss why it would be important to know what specific kinds of errors we make in terms of retrieving or recalling information?

2.   Discuss how the results from this lab could help you improve your memory for lists of items that have to be recalled in a specific order. Think in terms of attention.

Sternberg Search

Many researchers of memory believe that there exists a short-term memory (STM) system that holds information for a few seconds. If the information in STM is not transferred to long term memory (LTM) for more permanent storage, it vanishes. As evidence on the existence of STM grew, researchers started to explore its properties. In a series of articles starting in 1966 Saul Sternberg developed an experimental approach to explore how information was retrieved from STM.

The basic approach is simple. Subjects were shown a short (one to six items) list of numbers and asked to memorize them. After putting them to memory, a probe number was shown. The probe number was either one of the numbers in the list or a new number. The subject was to respond as quickly as possible whether the probe number was in the list or not. The reaction time of the subject should reflect the time spent searching STM to determine whether the probe number is part of the list. By varying the number of items in the list Sternberg hypothesized that he could test several theories of STM search.

For example, some types of neural network theories of memory suggest that every item in memory can be accessed simultaneously due to the parallel nature of search in these networks. If such a search took place in STM, one would expect the reaction times not to vary as number of items (memory set size) increased.

On the other hand, if memory search required consideration of each item in succession, the reaction times should increase with memory set size because the subject will, on average, have to search through more items. Sternberg's data was consistent with the successive (or serial) search.

Sternberg found two additional properties that were interesting. First, reaction times grew linearly with increases in memory set size. For each additional item in the memory set, subjects took (on average) an additional 38 milliseconds to make their response. Thus, it seems the probe item is compared one-by-one with each item in STM, and each comparison takes approximately 38 milliseconds.

Second, when he compared reaction times for probe "Present" and "Absent" trials (probe item was in the memory set or not, respectively), Sternberg found no differences in reaction times. This finding is notable because an "Absent" response can only be made after all items in STM have been searched and found to not match the probe item. At first glance it might seem that a "Present" trial could terminate as soon as the probe item is matched with the appropriate item in STM. As a result, with a self-terminating search, one would expect "Present" trials to be faster, but the data contradict this hypothesis.

The counterintuitive finding from Sternberg's study is that search of STM is always exhaustive. That is, the cognitive processes responsible for searching STM for a particular item search through all items in STM before reporting whether the probe item is in memory or not.

Sternberg's study and his analysis of the data had a major influence on models of memory and cognitive psychology in general. While more recent modeling approaches have shown that the implications of the data on theories of memory search are not as straightforward as once believed, the experimental approach and theorizing is classic. (For a recent review of the field see Van Zandt and Townsend, 1993). This experiment allows you to participate in a variation of the Sternberg memory search task.

For registration information go to http://coglab.wadsworth.com.

Start a trial by pressing the space bar. A fixation point will appear in the middle of the screen. After a second, a memory set consisting of 1, 3, or 5 numbers will appear on the screen for 1.2, 3.6, or 6 seconds, respectively. Study the numbers and commit them to memory. The memory set will disappear and then 1 to 3 seconds later a probe item will appear. Your task is to determine whether the probe item was in the list of just presented numbers. Respond as quickly as possible by pressing the / key (for "Present") or z key (for "Absent"). You will receive feedback on whether you were correct. When you are ready for the next trial, press the space bar again.

There is a minimum of 60 trials in the experimental session. For each "Present" and "Absent" condition 10 trials are presented for each memory set size. If you make a mistake (e.g., say the item was present when it was not), the trial will be repeated (with different numbers) later in the experiment. In this way, only reaction times where you were correct are used. If you find you are often making mistakes, you should try slowing down on your responses and/or try harder.

If you are distracted during a trial (e.g., you sneezed, attention drifted, you "zoned out") press the t key instead of z or /. This will discard the trial. Press the space bar to start the next trial. The discarded trial will be rerun later in the experiment.

When you finish the experiment, a window will appear that plots reaction time as a function of memory set size, with separate curves for "Present" and "Absent" trials. You should find that both curves increase with set size, and that the curves are nearly straight lines. Sternberg found that the "Present" and "Absent" curves were nearly superimposed, but you may not find that to be true (Sternberg's subjects had more practice and were paid to be highly motivated). Your data would agree with Sternberg's general findings if your curves were parallel. If your curves diverge as set size increases, your data is not consistent with Sternberg's general findings.

Additional References

Johns, E., & Mewhort, D. (2003). The effect of feature frequency on short-term recognition. *Memory & Cognition, 31*(2), 285-296.

Neubauer, A., Riemann, R., Mayer, R., & Angleitner, A. (1997). Intelligence and reaction times in the Hick, Sternberg, and Posner paradigms. *Personality & Individual Differences, 22*(6), 885-894.

Rojas, D., Teale, P., Sheeder, J., & Reite, M. (2000). Neuromagnetic alpha suppression during an auditory Sternberg task: Evidence for a serial, self-terminating search of short-term memory. *Cognitive Brain Research, 10*(1-2), 85-89.

Basic Questions

1. If your results showed that the two lines were parallel, and reaction times increased as the number of item increased, could you say that your data supported Sternberg's general findings?

2. What is the difference between serial and parallel processing?

3. If the neural network theories of memory were correct and we processed items in STM simultaneously due to the parallel nature of search in these networks, how would reaction times vary as the number of items increased?

4. How can the Sternberg Search task help to explain mental workload?

Advanced Questions

1. When using Sternberg's methodological design, results support a serial exhaustive search. Would you expect there to be any serial position effects in a serial exhaustive search? Why?

2. How could you apply Miller's theory of chunking to this CogLab? How could chunking be used in the Sternberg Search?

Discussion Questions

1. Discuss how reaction times would differ between the "present vs. absent" condition for the following theories - parallel search, serial-exhaustive search, serial-self-terminating search.

2. Discuss the likelihood that retrieval from short-term memory always involves a serial exhaustive search.

Suffix Effect

People often have to recall a series of items in order, such as when recalling a phone number. When the list of items is heard (as opposed to read silently), people usually are very good at remembering the final list item. However, if the list is followed by an irrelevant item (the suffix), recall of the final item is substantially impaired.

The suffix has to be perceived as speech in order for it to have a large effect. If the suffix is a pure tone, there is no impairment. Although the suffix has to be speech, it does not have to be a word. In general, the suffix will have a larger effect the more acoustically similar it is to the list items.

One reason that the suffix effect has attracted a lot of attention is that recall is impaired even when the suffix is expected and even when the suffix is the same item (usually the digit 0) on every trial.

The best explanation is that when the suffix is perceptually grouped with the list items, it functionally increases the list length. So, rather than trying to recall a 9 item list, you are in effect recalling a 10 item list (Neath, 1998).

For registration information go to http://coglab.wadsworth.com.

This lab requires a computer that can play sound. Before you start, please make sure that the volume of your computer/speakers is set to a comfortable level.

A few seconds after clicking on the start button, a window will appear with a blank screen on the left and buttons on the right. Start the experiment by clicking on the Next Trial button.

You will hear the digits 1-8 spoken in random order. On half the trials, you will hear a tone after the final item; on the remaining trials, you will hear the digit 0. After the tone or speech suffix has been presented, the response buttons will become active. Your task is to click on the buttons in the same order that the numbers were spoken. After you have finished clicking on all the buttons to recreate the list, click on 'Next Trial' to start the next sequence.

Being correct means that you click on the buttons in the same order the items appeared in the sequence. There is no way to change your response.

There are 30 trials, 15 suffix and 15 tone trials randomly intermixed.

When the experiment finishes, a new window will appear that gives the proportion of items you recalled at each list position in the speech suffix condition and in the tone suffix condition. You should do very well recalling the last item when it was followed by a tone, but you should do very poorly when the item was followed by a speech suffix.

119

Additional References

Pilotti, M., Beyer, T. & Yasunami, M. (2002). Top-down processing and the suffix effect in young and older adults. *Memory & Cognition, 30* (1).

Surprenant, A. M., LeCompte, D. C., & Neath, I. (2000). Manipulations of irrelevant information: Suffix effects with articulatory suppression and irrelevant speech. *Quarterly Journal of Experimental Psychology, 53A*, 325-348.

Basic Questions

1. If the "0" on the end of the list of words was predictable, meaning it happened every time, do you think it would it still affect your memory? Why or why not?

2. How did the added suffix at the end of list affect your memory for the list of words? How did the tone affect your memory for the list?

3. You are talking to your friend on his CB radio about a great party that he knows about. He tells you to call him on his new cell phone if you need a ride because you are not sure where it is and he proceeds to quickly give you his number – 6-4-7-5-3-6-5. As you repeat the number back to yourself, you hear your friend on the other end say "10-4 good buddy" and the line goes dead. How did he mess up your ability to remember his phone number?

4. Somehow you find yourself being dragged to a charity bingo game hosted by your sorority. Half way through a game you have to excuse yourself to make an important phone call. When you return to the table, your friends tell you that they missed blotting out the numbers that were just called on your cards, but they proceed to quickly recite the numbers that were called while you were gone – 3-52-35-7-41-23-15 and 21. As you reach for your bingo dabber, the caller yells "Under the B-10" and you forget all of the numbers that you were repeating to yourself. Would this have happened if the number 10 was visually displayed, while a bell sounded to direct attention towards a board that had all the called numbers lit up on it?

5. It is Thanksgiving and you are having dinner with your new boyfriend's family, his very large family. Before sitting down at a huge dinner table, he begins introducing you to his family. After giving you about ten names to remember, his nephew brings up this cute puppy and tells you his name is "Roger". When you sit down to eat, you look out at the strange faces and you can only remember the first three and then you draw a blank. How did "Roger" affect your memory?

Advanced Questions

1. There are two main ideas about how we filter information from our environments. According to one theory, we filter late, meaning we take in all information and then decide if we need to use it for our response. The other idea is that we filter early or we take in only a certain amount of information and block the rest. Decide which of these two competing theories best explains the results of this CogLab? Why?

2. According to the serial position curve, memory for the beginning (primacy effect) and the end of a list (recency effect) seems to be better than memory for information in the middle of a list. What would the added suffix do for each of this phenomenon in terms of memory recall?

3. If visually presented stimuli did not show a similar interference effect on memory recall compared to verbally presented material, what could be said about the differences between the memory stores for each of the methods of presentation?

Discussion Questions

1. If your professor told you that the Suffix Effect was stronger in verbally presented material than in visually presented information, what suggestions would you have for your other teachers when presenting class materials?

2. We know that we have limited resources when it comes to such cognitive activities like memory. Discuss possible tricks that you use to improve your memory for important information?

6.1 EPISODIC MEMORY AND SEMANTIC MEMORY

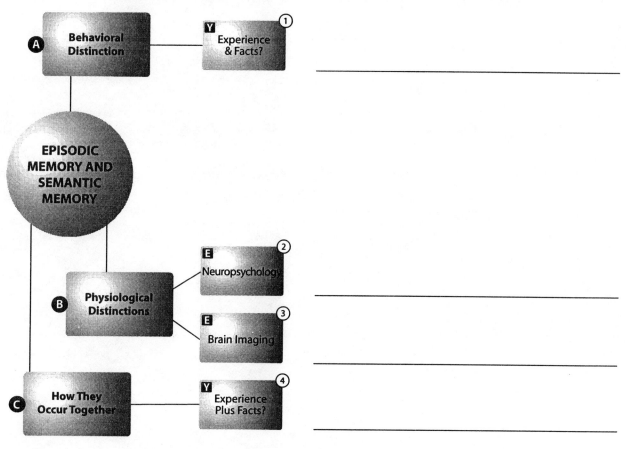

A What is the distinction between episodic memory and semantic memory?

① **Your Experience:** Think about a few of the things you know or have experienced and classify each of these things as episodic or semantic memories.

B How can physiological research help distinguish between episodic and semantic memory?

② **Experiment (Neuropsychology):** Describe two patients with poor episodic memory and intact semantic memory, and one patient with intact episodic memory and poor semantic memory. What kind of a dissociation do these patients, taken together, represent? (Schacter; Vargha-Khadem; DeRenzi; 186)

③ **Experiment:** How has brain imaging distinguished between episodic and semantic memory? (Duzel; 188)

C How can episodic and semantic information occur together?

④ **Your Experience:** Describe a situation in which your memory for an experience (episodic) may have been influenced by factual knowledge (semantic).

6.2 IMPLICIT MEMORY

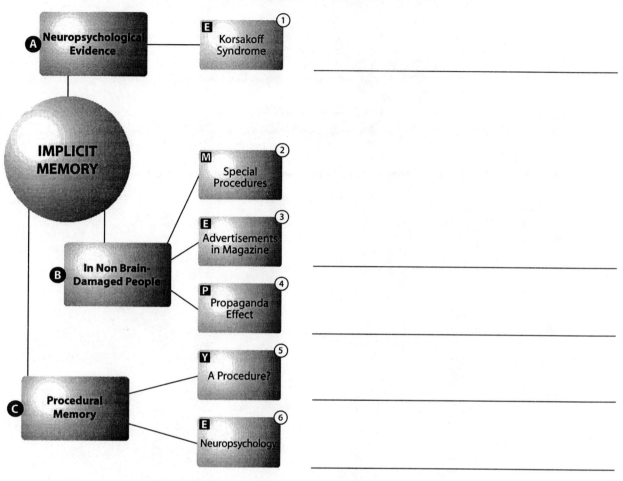

A How can the behavior of people with brain damage demonstrate implicit memory?

① **Experiment (Neuropsychology):** What is implicit memory? How do the results of experiments, in which Korsakoff's patients are asked to identify fragmented pictures, demonstrate implicit memory? (Warrington & Weiskrantz; 189)

B How can implicit memory be demonstrated in people without brain damage?

② **Method:** What is repetition priming? What procedures are used to prevent non brain-damaged participants from remembering the initial presentation of a priming stimulus? (191)

③ **Experiment:** Describe the experiment that demonstrated implicit memory for advertisements in a magazine (Perfect & Askew; 191)

④ **Principle:** What is the propaganda effect? Why is it important? (192)

C What is a kind of memory that doesn't involve remembering events or facts?

⑤ **Your Experience:** What are some motor skills and some cognitive skills that would be examples of procedural memory?

⑥ **Experiment (Neuropsychology):** How did Schacter's golf partner, who had Alzheimers, illustrate procedural memory? (192)

6.3 STORING INFORMATION IN LONG-TERM MEMORY I

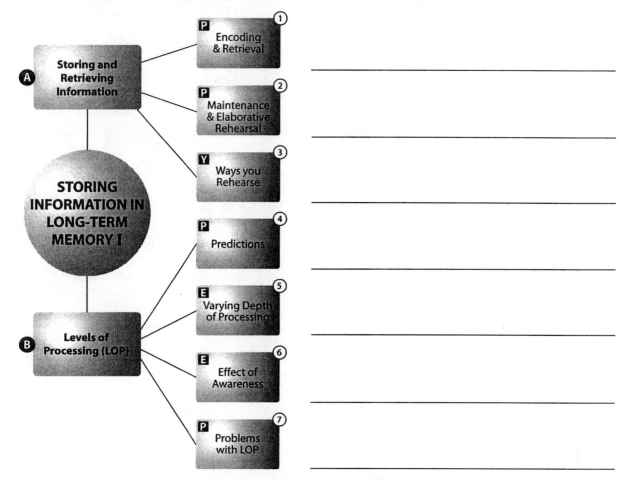

A How does information get into LTM, and how is it then "withdrawn"?

1. **Principle:** What is encoding and how is it distinguished from "coding"? What is retrieval? (193)
2. **Principle:** Define maintenance rehearsal and elaborative rehearsal. Which is a more effective way to establish information in LTM? (193)
3. **Your experience:** Describe a situation in which you have used maintenance rehearsal and another situation in which you have used elaborative rehearsal. Why did you use different types of rehearsal in the two situations?

B What are the characteristics of levels of processing theory?

4. **Principle:** What two predictions does levels of processing theory make? (195)
5. **Experiment:** How was depth of processing varied for the demonstration in which words were presented in lists and for the experiment in which participants answered questions about words? How did memory differ for deep processing and shallow processing? (Craik & Tulving; 195)
6. **Experiment:** Describe the experiment that investigated the effect of telling participants that they were going to be given a memory test. (Hyde & Jenkins; 196)
7. **Principle:** What are some criticisms of levels of processing theory? (196)

6.4 STORING INFORMATION IN LONG-TERM MEMORY II

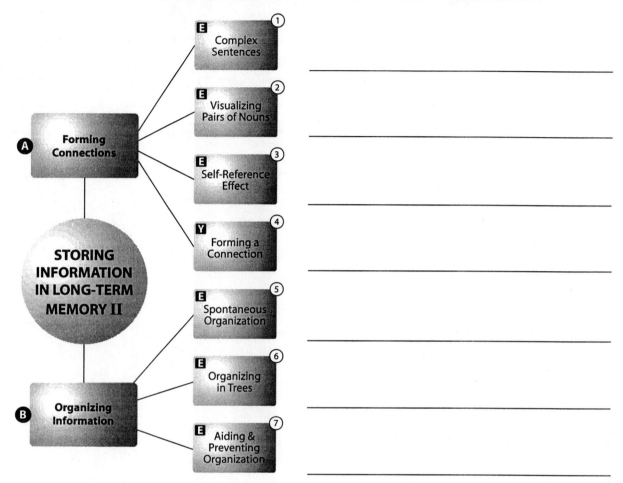

A **How does forming connections between words affect memory?**

① **Experiment:** How does presenting words in a complex sentence affect memory? (Craik & Tulving; 197)

② **Experiment:** How does creating visual images based on pairs of nouns affect memory for the words? (Bower & Winzenz; 197)

③ **Experiment:** What is the self-reference effect? How did an experiment demonstrate its effect on memory? How can this effect be described in terms of (a) depth of processing and (b) retrieval cues? (Rogers; 198)

④ **Your Experience:** Describe a situation in which you were able to remember something by forming a "connection". If you can't think of an example, think of a situation in which you might use this technique.

B **How does organizing information affect memory?**

⑤ **Experiment:** Describe the demonstration that showed that people spontaneously organize words as they are recalled. (Jenkins & Russell; 200)

⑥ **Experiment:** Describe the experiment that investigated how presenting words in an organized "tree" affects memory. (Bower; 200)

⑦ **Experiment:** Describe the "balloon" experiment. What was the point of this experiment? (Bransford & Johnson; 201)

6.5 MEMORY & THE BRAIN

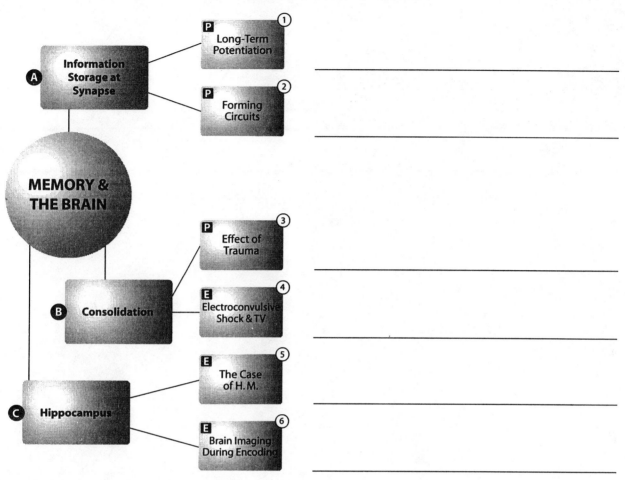

A How are memories stored at synapses?

① **Principle:** Describe Hebb's idea about how memories can be represented by physiological changes at the synapse. How is this idea supported by long-term potentiation? (203)

② **Principle:** Describe how connections between two things can be established by neural circuits. (205)

B Why are memories sometimes disrupted by traumatic events, like a blow to the head?

③ **Principle:** What kind of amnesia occurs when memory is disrupted by a blow to the head? How is this phenomenon related to memory consolidation? (206)

④ **Experiment:** What did the experiment that measured memory for TV programs show about memory consolidation? (Squire; 206)

C What is the role of the hippocampus in episodic memory?

⑤ **Experiment (Neuropsychology):** Describe the case of H. M. What did the memory capacities that he lost and those that remained indicate about the role of the hippocampus in memory? (Milner; 207)

⑥ **Experiment:** How do the results of brain imaging experiments show how the brain activity that occurs during encoding is related to later memory? (Brewer; Davachi; 207)

A **How is the ability to retrieve memories affected by retrieval cues?**

① **Principle:** What does the author's experience in forgetting a video and his student's experience upon returning to her grandparents' house illustrate about memory retrieval? (209)

② **Experiment:** How does providing category "cues" affect performance on a memory test? Why does this occur? (Tulving & Pearlstone; 210)

③ **Experiment:** Describe the experiment in which participants were presented with a list of 600 nouns. What do the results indicate about the best way to establish retrieval cues? (Mantyla; 210)

④ **Your experience:** Describe a situation in which a retrieval cue helped you remember something.

B **What is transfer-appropriate processing?**

⑤ **Experiment:** Describe the semantic/rhyming experiment. What are the implications of the results of this experiment for levels of processing theory? (Morris; 212)

6.7 RETRIEVING INFORMATION FROM LONG-TERM MEMORY II

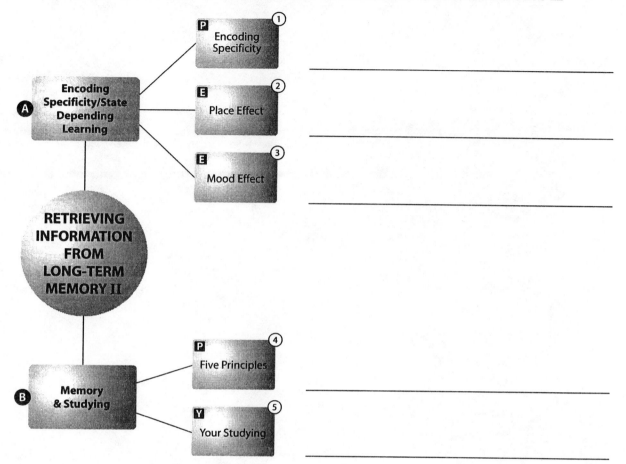

A **How does encoding specificity affect memory?**

① **Principle:** What is the principle of encoding specificity? How does the principle of state-dependent learning follow from encoding specificity? (213)

② **Experiments:** Describe the "diving" and "studying" experiments that demonstrated state-dependent learning for place. (Godden & Baddeley; Grant; 214)

③ **Experiment:** Describe the experiment that showed how mood can affect memory. (Eich & Metcalfe; 216)

B **How can the principles of memory be used to improve the effectiveness of studying?**

④ **Principle:** What are five memory principles that can be applied to studying? (216)

⑤ **Your Experience:** Analyze your own studying in terms of the "five principles". Based on this analysis, think of things you could do to improve the effectiveness of your studying.

Implicit Learning

The term implicit learning refers to "the process by which knowledge about the rule-governed complexities of the stimulus environment is acquired independently of conscious attempts to do so" (Reber, 1989, p. 219).

One form of implicit learning involves serial pattern learning. In this task, subjects are asked to press one of four keys as quickly as they can whenever they see an stimulus, such as an asterisk, appear in any of four locations (labeled A, B, C, and D). If the asterisk appears in location A, the subject is asked to press (for example) the "z" key. If the asterisk appears in location B, the subject is asked to press the "x" key. There is an underlying pattern that defines the order of locations. It is this pattern that the subject will learn.

As the sequence is repeated, subjects press the keys more quickly. This indicates that learning has taken place. More evidence comes from a transfer test, in which the pattern is changed (again, without telling the subject). Now, the subjects press the keys much more slowly.

The key evidence to support the idea that learning is implicit -- not conscious -- comes from tests in which subjects are asked what the pattern was. The typical finding is that subjects are unaware of the pattern, but their behavior shows that they have nonetheless learned it (see Stadler & Frensch, 1998).

This demonstration is modeled on a study reported by Destrebecqz & Cleeremans (2001). There will be a long series of trials in which you will be asked to indicate the location of a circle. Please try to respond as quickly as you possibly can. At the end of the experiment, you will be asked what the rule was that determined the circle's location.

For registration information go to http://coglab.wadsworth.com.

Start a block of trials by pressing the space bar. You will see a circle appear in one of four locations. Your task is to indicate the location of the circle by pressing the appropriate key as quickly as you can.

What follows are more detailed instructions.

After clicking on the experiment, a window will appear. Start a trial by pressing the space bar. A short time later, a circle will appear in one of the four locations shown below. Your task is to indicate the location of the circle by pressing the appropriate key as quickly as you can.

- If the circle appears in the left-most location, press the "z" key as quickly as you can.
- If the circle appears in the second location, press the "x" key as quickly as you can.
- If the circle appears in the third location, press the "." key as quickly as you can.
- If the circle appears in the right-most location, press the "/" key as quickly as you can.

Place your left index finger on the "x" key and your right index finger on the "." key. Place your left middle finger on the "z" key and your right middle finger on the "/" key.

If the '.' and '/' keys are not the right-most keys on your keyboard, you can use the Instructions menu that will appear once you start the demo. There are 288 trials (each trial takes only a few seconds), and you can take a rest every 24 trials. Press the space bar to start each trial.

At the end of the experiment a new window will appear that reports the mean reaction time (RT) in milliseconds for each block of 24 trials. You should find that your mean RT decreases with each block. On Block 10, you should find a sudden increase in mean RT because that block uses a different pattern. Blocks 11 and 12 go back to the first pattern. Before you look at the results window, try to write down what the pattern was that determined the order of the locations. Then, compare your "rule" with the one provided in the window. You should find that your "rule" is incorrect even though your RTs show that you learned the rule!

Additional References

Advertising
Shapiro, S. & Krishnan, H. (2001). Memory-based measures for assessing advertising effects: A comparison of explicit and implicit memory effects. *Journal of Advertising, 30* (3).

Development
Vinter, A. & Perruchet, P. (2000). Implicit learning in children is not related to age: Evidence from drawing behavior. *Child Development, 71* (5), 1223.

Motor skills
Pohl, P., McDowd, J., Filion, D., Richards, L. & Stiers, W. (2001). Implicit learning of a perceptual-motor skill after a stroke. *Physical Therapy, 81*, 1780-1790.

Amnesia
Curran, T. (1997). Higher-order associative learning in amnesia: Evidence from the serial reaction time task. *Journal of Cognitive Neuroscience, 9*(4), 522-534.

Basic Questions

1. If the results show that the mean reaction times gradually decreased from block 1 to block 12, what could you imply was happening?

2. Indicate which of the following examples would be explained through explicit or implicit learning. Just write explicit or implicit in the space provided.
    a) Driving a standard vehicle _____
    b) Arriving 10 minutes late to a class where you know the professor is usually 15 minutes late

    _____
    c) Being able to sing along with your favorite song, but not being able to write out the words

    _____

d) Answering these questions _____

e) You have trouble writing down directions to your Grandmother's house, but you are able to drive there with no problems _____

3. Through Classical Conditioning, a neutral stimulus, like cologne, can elicit or bring about a positive emotional response when we learn to associate it with someone we like, for example our boyfriend or girlfriend. How can this association be explained in terms of implicit learning?

4. Your friends are talking about a song that you insist you do not know. Even after hearing part of the song, you still don't recognize it. When the chorus comes along, however, you start to sing the words. Now your friends think you were lying to them. How could you explain this behavior using implicit learning?

5. While driving to school, you stop to give your friend a ride. While driving, your friend asks why you take the Hospital route when University Avenue is faster. You really don't know why you take the Hospital route, but you have been doing it since last year around Christmas time. Could implicit learning be used to explain why you take the longer route? What if you remembered that there had been construction on University Avenue that began around Christmas time that held up traffic going to the University?

6. How do advertising companies use the concept of implicit learning when designing their client's commercials?

Advanced Questions

1. In a recent Hollywood film, *Momento,* the main character received a blow to the head and developed Anterograde amnesia. The main character in the movie could not form new long-term memories and he lost all personal memories from the time of the accident to the present, however, he could use a telephone, drive his sports car, walk and talk. From this information, what would you suspect about the type of memory loss related to Anterograde amnesia?

2. Do you think the idea of having two separate memory stores or at least two aspects of one main memory system important to understanding human behavior?

3. How can implicit learning be used to possibly explain an addiction to alcohol?

Discussion Questions

1. Give 3 specific examples of odd behaviors you exhibit and then think about possible explanations for these behaviors. Use the concepts of implicit and explicit learning to answer this question.

2. How would implicit memory be related to some psychological disorders, like obsessive-compulsive disorder, bipolar (or other mood disorders), eating disorders or anxiety disorders? Discuss specific behaviors related to the disorder and how learning could allow the abnormal behavior to continue.

Encoding Specificity

According to the encoding specificity principle (Tulving, 1983) the recollection of an event depends on the interaction between the properties of the encoded event and the properties of the encoded retrieval information. In other words, whether an item will be remembered at a particular time depends on the interaction between the processing that occurred during encoding and the processing that occurs at retrieval.

This principle has important implications for what you can say about memory. Because it is the interaction of both encoding and retrieval that is important, it means that you cannot make any statement about the mnemonic properties of an item or a type of processing or a cue unless you specify both the encoding and the retrieval conditions (Tulving, 1983). Thus, you cannot say things like:

- Recognition is easier than recall
- Deep processing is better than shallow processing
- Pictures are recalled better than words

These statements are all meaningless because the encoding and retrieval conditions are not mentioned. It is easy to create situations in which recall is easier than recognition, shallow processing leads to better memory than deep processing, and words are recalled better than pictures.

This demo is based on Thomson and Tulving (1970). Some target words will be presented alone at study and some will be presented along with a weak cue. At test, there are three cue conditions: no cue, a weak cue, or a strong cue. A strong cue is a word that elicits a particular target word most of the time. For example, when most people hear the word DOG, the first word that pops into their head is CAT. A weak cue is a word that only rarely elicits a particular target. When people hear EYE, they respond with CAT only about 1% of the time. A reasonable prediction seems to be that strong cues should be better than weak cues at eliciting the correct item. However, this inference is not valid because it fails to take into account the relationship between the encoding and retrieval conditions.

For registration information go to http://coglab.wadsworth.com.

There are two phases to this demo. Phase I. Start Phase I by pressing the space bar. You will see a series of words; each is shown on the screen for approximately 3 seconds. Some will be shown by themselves, and some as word pairs. For example, you might see: hand-PALM, or you might just see -PALM. The memory test in Phase II will always ask bout the word in UPPERCASE. After all the words have been shown, you will be in Phase II. You will be asked to judge whether the target word was one of the uppercase words you saw in Phase I.

Sometimes you will see a target word shown by itself, and sometimes you will see it paired with a cue. For each uppercase word, press 'Y' to indicate YES you did remember seeing the word in Phase I; press

'N' to indicate that NO, you do not remember seeing the word. Press the space bar to start each test trial. There are 48 words shown in Phase I and 96 trials in Phase II.

The summary results show the proportion of times you responded Y (you remembered seeing the uppercase word during Phase I) to each of the nine conditions. You should find that when there was no cue present at study, you did best when there was a strong cue at test than either a weak cue or no cue. However, when there was a weak cue at study, you should find that the weak cue at test led to better performance than the strong cue. The important aspect of this result is that the effectiveness of even a long-standing strong cue depends crucially on the processes which occurred at study.

Additional References

Martin, E. (1975). Generation-recognition theory and the encoding specificity principle. *Psychological Review, 82*, 150-153.

Thomson, D. M., & Tulving, E. (1970). Associative encoding and retrieval: Weak and strong cues. *Journal of Experimental Psychology, 86*, 255-262

Tulving, E., & Thomson, D. M. (1973). Encoding specificity and retrieval processes in episodic memory. *Psychological Review, 80*, 352-373.

Tulving, E. (1983). *Elements of episodic memory*. New York: Oxford University Press.

Basic Questions

1. Why do you think that having a weak cue at the test phase improves the memory for a word that had a weak cue at study compared to a strong cue?

2. You are having trouble remembering your high school prom, although you know that you had a good time and it has only been 2 years. What could you do to try to remember your prom night?

3. While walking your dog, you see a strange dog running around. You think you remember seeing this dog before but you are not sure. As you round the corner, you run into a woman from your neighborhood that is looking for her dog. You suddenly remember that you saw that woman walking that strange dog you saw earlier in the week. What was missing when you were trying to remember if you recognized the stray dog?

4. While shopping for new cologne for your father for Christmas, you smell something that you recognize but you can't remember what the smell is. You find that you are having memory flashbacks of sitting around a fire and drinking apple cider with friends. As you look around, you notice a candle burning and you recognize that as the smell you detected. Explain how a candle, you have never seen before, could be related to the memory flashbacks with your friends.

5. You are a huge fraternity party and you see a girl playing beach volleyball that you think you

recognize but you are not sure. You are not able to talk to her but it bugs you that you can't remember where you know her from. On Monday morning as you walk into Biology class, you see that same girl sitting in front of you. You feel a bit stupid that you didn't remember her from the party because she has sat in front of you for 2 months now. Now that you have done this lab, how would you explain you memory problem?

Advanced Questions

1. While taking your psychology test, you notice that the girl beside you is singing a song about the different brain parts. After doing this lab, what could you infer about her encoding methods during her studying?

2. You find out that on the morning of the test that the classroom has been changed from your regular classroom to a room that you have never been in. How do you think this will affect your test performance?

3. Your mother is making your favorite pie for dessert, but she ran out of ingredients and asks you to go to the store for her. She only needs eggs, milk, white sugar and cinnamon, so you don't write it down. When you get to the store, you remember the milk, cinnamon and sugar but can't remember what the last thing was. Just then, a woman walks in and she is wearing the same shirt that your mother was wearing and you suddenly remember the eggs. How did the woman's shirt help you remember the eggs?

Discussion Questions

1. Now that you know that the environment and conditions of learning plays an important role on memory recall or recognition, discuss some of the important factors to keep in mind if you were trying to study more effectively for a test.

2. Discuss how encoding specificity could be used to explain why using self-referent examples improve memory for to-be-learned material. Discuss any possible drawbacks with using your own examples over ones that teachers provide for you.

7.1 AUTOBIOGRAPHICAL MEMORY

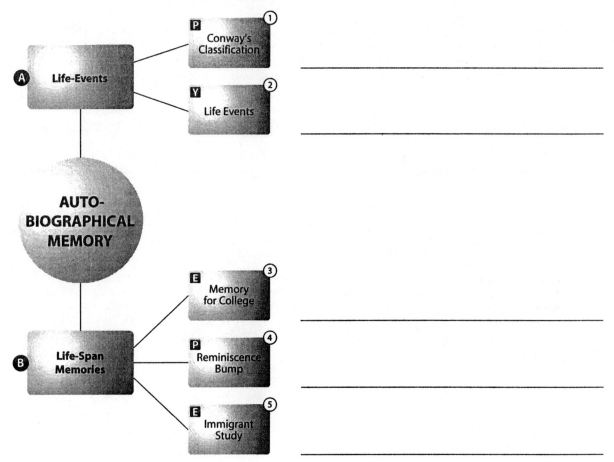

A   **What is autobiographical memory?**

①   **Principle:** How can autobiographical memories be described in terms of three "layers of knowledge"? (225)

②   **Your Experience:** Classify some events in your life in terms of Conway's idea of "layers of knowledge".

B   **What determines which life-events we will remember?**

③   **Experiment:** What were the results of the survey of the memories of Wellesley College students? (Pillemer; 226)

④   **Principle:** What is the reminiscence bump? How was it determined? What two hypotheses have been proposed to explain it? (227)

⑤   **Experiment:** Describe the "immigrant" study. What does it demonstrate about the reminiscence bump? (Schrauf & Rubin; 228)

7.2 FLASHBULB MEMORY

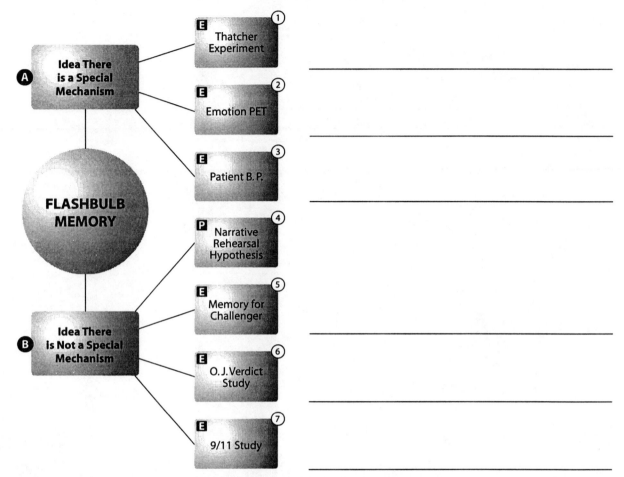

A **Is there a special mechanism for flashbulb memories?**

① **Experiment:** Describe the experiment in which British and U.S. participants were asked to remember the day British Prime Minister Thatcher resigned. What was the point of this experiment? (Conway; 229)

② **Experiment:** What did a PET study indicate about brain activation and memory? (Hamann; 229)

③ **Experiment (Neuropsychology):** What structure was damaged in B.P.'s brain, and what effect did this have on his memory for emotional parts of a story? (Cahill; 230)

B **What evidence argues against a special mechanism for flashbulb memories?**

④ **Principle:** What is the narrative rehearsal hypothesis? (230)

⑤ **Experiment:** What do the results of the "Challenger" experiment indicate about the accuracy of flashbulb memories? (Neisser & Harsch; 231)

⑥ **Experiment:** What do the results of the O.J. Simpson verdict experiment indicate about the decay of "flashbulb" memories? (Schmolck; 232)

⑦ **Experiment:** What do the results of the 9/11 study indicate about flashbulb memories? (Talarico & Rubin; 232)

7.3 CONSTRUCTIVE NATURE OF MEMORY I

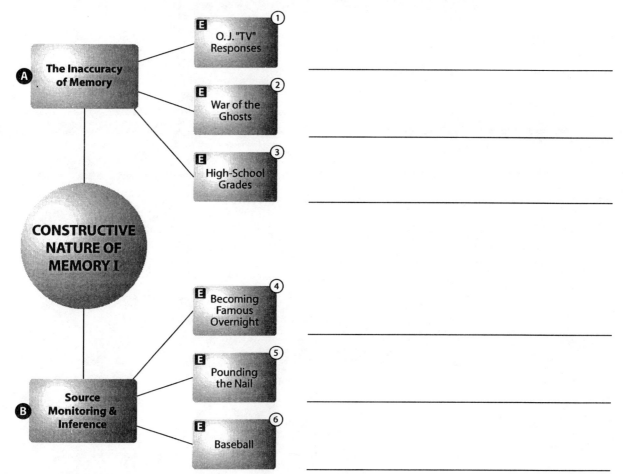

A   **What is the evidence that we construct inaccurate memories?**

①   **Experiment:** What result from the O.J. Simpson verdict study supports the idea that memories are constructed? (Schmolck; 234)

②   **Experiment:** Describe the "War of the Ghosts" experiment. What technique did it introduce and what were the implications of its results? (Bartlett; 235)

③   **Experiment:** What does the experiment about memory for high school grades indicate about memory? (Bahrick; 236)

B   **What is source monitoring and how does inference affect memory?**

④   **Experiment:** Describe the "becoming famous overnight" experiment. What does it indicate about source monitoring? (Jacoby; 237)

⑤   **Experiment:** What does the "pounding the nail" experiment indicate about the role of inference in perception? (Bransford & Johnson; 238)

⑥   **Experiment:** What does the "baseball" experiment indicate about the role of past experience on inference? (Arkes & Freedman; 239)

7.4 CONSTRUCTIVE NATURE OF MEMORY II

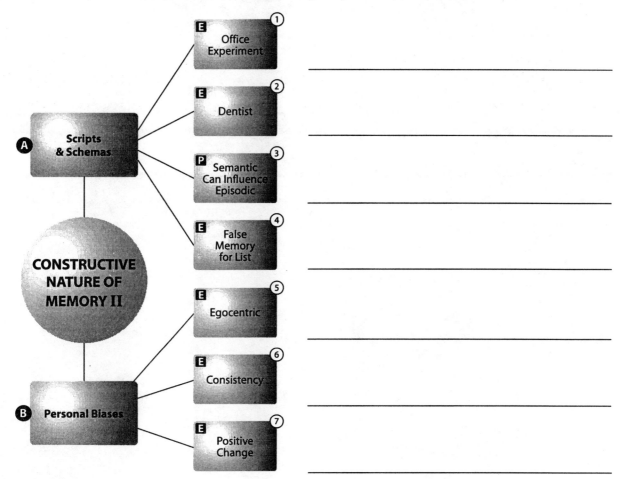

(A) **What is a script? A schema?**

① **Experiment:** What does the experiment in which participants were asked what they saw in an office demonstrate about how schemas can affect memory? (Brewer & Treyens; 240)

② **Experiment:** What does the "dentist" experiment demonstrate about how scripts can affect memory? (Bower; 240)

③ **Principle:** Describe how the results of the office and dentist experiments demonstrate how semantic memory can influence episodic memory. (242)

④ **Experiment:** How does the demonstration that tested memory for a list of words illustrate false memory? (Deese; 242)

(B) **How do personal biases affect memory?**

⑤ **Experiment:** How does the extravert/introvert experiment illustrate the egocentric bias? (Sanitiosco; 243)

⑥ **Experiment:** How does the experiment that tested people's attitudes at two different times illustrate the effect of the consistency bias on memory? (Marcus; 243)

⑦ **Experiment:** How does the experiment in which couples were surveyed about their relationships illustrate the positive change bias? (Sprecher; 244)

7.5 SUGGESTIBILITY OF MEMORY

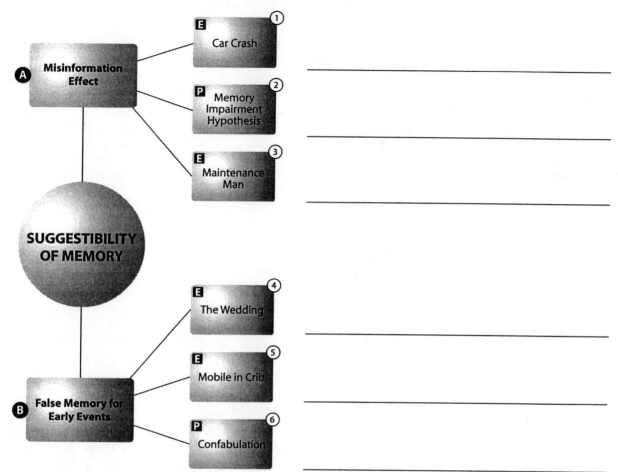

A What is the misinformation effect and what is the mechanism behind it?

① **Experiment:** Describe the two "car crash" experiments, which demonstrated the effect of misleading post-event information. (Loftus; Loftus & Palmer; 248)

② **Principle:** What is the memory impairment hypothesis and how does it apply to the results of the car crash experiments? (248)

③ **Experiment:** Describe the "maintenance man" experiment. How do the results argue against the memory impairment hypothesis? (McClosky & Zaragoza; 250)

B Can false memories be created for early experiences?

④ **Experiment:** Describe the "wedding" experiment. How did the participant's responses compare for the first and second interviews? What probably caused the response to change for the second interview? (Hyman; 251)

⑤ **Experiment:** Describe the "mobile in crib" experiment. What does it demonstrate about false memories for events that occurred in infancy? (DuBreiul; 252)

⑥ **Principle:** Describe the confabulation that can occur in cases of brain damage. What does the confabulation caused by brain damage tell us about normal memory? (252)

7.6 EYEWITNESS TESTIMONY & MEMORY

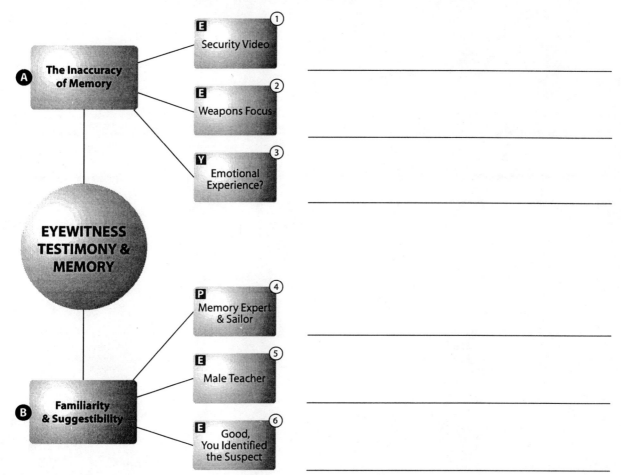

A How accurate is eyewitness testimony?

① **Experiment:** What happened when participants were asked to identify the gunman they had seen in a security video? (Wells & Bradfield; 255)

② **Experiment:** What is weapons focus and how was it demonstrated in an experiment? (Stany & Johnson; 255)

③ **Your Experience:** Can you think of a situation in which the "emotionality" of an event may have affected your memory for that event?

B How can "familiarity" lead to the creation of false memories?

④ **Principle:** What do the examples of the memory researcher and the sailor, both of whom were misidentified by eyewitnesses, demonstrate about the effect of familiarity on memory? (256)

⑤ **Experiment:** Describe the experiment in which a male teacher was erroneously picked from a photo spread. What does the result of this experiment demonstrate? (Ross; 256)

⑥ **Experiment:** Describe the "Good, you identified the suspect" experiment. What does the result of this experiment demonstrate about the effect of feedback on memory? (Wells & Bradfield; 258)

Remember / Know

In a typical test of recognition memory, a subject might be shown a test item and asked whether it was one that was presented on a particular list. The target can be either old -- it was on the list -- or new -- it was not on the list. If the subject decides that an old test item was on the list that is called a hit. If the subject decides that a new test item was on the list, this is called a false alarm.

A relatively recent change in testing recognition memory has been the introduction of the Remember/Know paradigm (Tulving, 1985). When subjects judge an item to be old, they are asked to make a further distinction. If they are consciously aware of some aspects of the original episode, then they should indicate that they remember the item. For example, they can remember a particular thought that the word triggered, or they can remember thinking it was a coincidence that this particular word followed the previous one. If they have no conscious awareness of the learning episode, then they should respond that they just know that the item was on the list.

The distinction can be explained in a different way. If you were asked, "Who was the first President of the United States?", you most likely would name George Washington. However, you probably do not consciously recollect the original episode during which you learned this information. Rather, you just know the answer. In contrast, consider the following statement; Abraham Lincoln's first vice-president was Hannibal Hamlin, who was born in Paris, Maine. If, later on, someone asks you, "Who was Abraham Lincoln's first vice-president?" - you might answer with Hannibal Hamlin. If you were consciously aware that you first learned this fact while reading a web page on CogLab, then you would remember this information in the remember/know sense. Note that it is not the type of information that makes a difference; rather, it is the presence or absence of conscious awareness of aspects of the prior experience.

This demonstration replicates studies reported by Gardiner (1988) and Rajaram (1993). You will be shown a series of words, and asked to generate either a synonym or a word that rhymes. Then you will be given a recognition test, in which you will be asked to indicate whether you recognize the word.

For registration information go to http://coglab.wadsworth.com.

Press the space bar to start each trail. There are two phases. You will need a blank sheet of paper and a pen for the first phase. In Phase I, you will see a word and an instruction. If the instruction says Synonym, write down a word that has the same meaning as the word shown. If the instruction says Rhyme, write down a word that sounds the same as the target word. When you are done, press the space bar for the next item. You will need to write down your work quickly: each item is shown for only 5 seconds.

After this, you'll enter Phase II. Press the space bar to start each trial. You will be shown a series of words, half of which were shown in Phase I, and half of which are new words. Please answer the question, Was this word in Phase I? If it was, decide whether you remember the word or simply know it was on the list. Press 'R' to indicate remember, and 'K' to indicate know. If the word was not on the list, press the 'N' key.

The judgment remember means that you are consciously aware of the learning episode: you can recollect some aspect of the experience, such as the word you provided as a synonym or rhyme, or the word that came before, or your thoughts about the word. If can't recollect such information, then you should choose know.

There are 80 words shown in Phase I, and 160 trials in Phase II.

When the experiment is over, you will see a table that shows how accurate you were in recognizing which items were on the original list. For the items that you said were on the list, you will also see the proportion of remember and know judgments made. You should give more remember than know judgments to words that you generated synonyms for, and you should give fewer remember and more know judgments to words that you generated rhymes for.

Additional References

Arnold, M. M., & Lindsay, D. S. (2002). Remembering remembering. *Journal of Experimental Psychology: Learning, Memory, and Cognition, 28*, 521-529.

Hyman, I. E., Jr., Gilstrap, L. L., Decker, K., & Wilkinson, C. (1998). Manipulating remember and know judgments of autobiographical memories: An investigation of false memory creation. *Applied Cognitive Psychology, 12*, 371-386.

Basic Questions

1. Why do you think "remembering" was related to the synonym condition & rhyming was related to "knowing?

2. When doing this lab, which task took longer to do, on average, coming up with a synonym or a rhyme?

3. Your friend just got a brand new sports car for his birthday and he said you could test drive it. All excited, you jump into the driver's seat and you notice that it is a standard. It has been a long time since you drove a standard. If you find you are talking yourself through the steps necessary to drive the standard as your father once told you, what kind of memory are you displaying and why?

4. During your psychology final exam you find you aren't really thinking very hard and you get through the multiple choice questions very quickly. You are the first one finished and although this worries you, you decide to leave to study for another final you have that afternoon. When you get your grade back for that test you see that you received a 90%. What kind of recognition memory was helping you through the test that quickly?

5. While at the mall, you see someone that you recognize, although you can't place why you recognize her. As she gets closer to you, you hear her talking to a friend about playing in a band and you realize that she works at a music store near your house. How did knowing her change to remembering her?

Advanced Questions

1. You go into your favorite restaurant for supper and before you sit down, the waiter brings you an iced tea, your usual and favorite drink of choice. How could you test what kind of recognition memory the waiter was using when he brought you the tea?

2. Exams are over and you and your roommates decide to rent a movie to unwind and de-stress. They pick out a movie that you are positive that you haven't seen. As you start to watch the movie, something happens and you suddenly get excited because you know what the movie is all about. What has just happened to you?

3. Your roommate always sings in the shower and in the car on the way to school. In the shower, he just sings the songs from memory (no radio playing), but in the car, he sings along with the radio, even with those songs that he doesn't know very well. Although he knows the words, he rarely knows what the words mean. Sometimes he makes more errors when he is familiar with the song. In terms of his memory, what could be happening?

Discussion Questions

1. Discuss any possible effects that level of <u>concreteness</u> or <u>abstractness</u> may play in your ability to "remember" a concept or "know" a concept. Talk about why this makes sense and use examples to support your answer.

2. One area of interest to memory researchers is the ability to manipulate memories through priming or leading. Discuss how this lab could contribute to the manipulation of "remembering" and "knowing" a memory. One of the references provided includes a study of manipulations of autobiographical memories.

False Memory

An important issue for theories of cognition is how well we remember things. It is important because nearly every aspect of cognition depends on memory to some degree. To understand problem solving, decision making, attention, and perception, one needs to know the abilities and limits of memory. The quality of memory is important for practical reasons as well. Many significant events depend on reports from human observers. From eyewitness testimony in murder trials to arguments with a spouse about who said what, memory, and memory accuracy, is critical. A surprising finding is that there is no way to assess memory accuracy without objective evidence (like a tape recording or a photograph). The vividness or confidence of the person recalling the memory is not an accurate indication of the truth of the memory. This is not to say that most memories are inaccurate; we must be pretty accurate much of the time or else living would be quite difficult. However, for those situations where accuracy of detail is important, memories cannot be trusted, no matter how adamant the recaller is about the vividness of the memory.

This experiment demonstrates one methodology that biases people to recall things that did not occur. The memories associated with experiments of this type are often called false memories. The method was first used by Deese (1959) and has been extended more recently by Roediger and McDermott (1995). The task is like many other memory experiments. A sequence of words is presented (verbally or visually) and the observer is to subsequently classify a set of words as either in the sequence (old) or not in the sequence (new).

What differentiates this experiment from other memory experiments is that the sequences are specially designed to bias observers to report a particular word that was not included in the list. When people report that one of these words was in the sequence, but it really was not, they are having a false memory. In some cases people will report that they vividly recall seeing (or hearing) the word, so their memory is very strong, despite its inaccuracy.

For registration information go to http://coglab.wadsworth.com.

After clicking on the start button, a window will appear with a blank area on the left and a number of buttons on the right. Start a trial by pressing the Next trial button. On the left of the window a sequence of words will appear, with each word presented for one and a half seconds. After the full sequence has been presented, the buttons on the right will show labels for words, including some of those just shown. The other buttons will contain distractor words. You must distinguish the old words from the new, distractor, words. Your task is to click on the buttons for the words that were just shown. Not all the words in the sequence will be listed on the buttons. After you have finished clicking on all the buttons that you remember being in the sequence, click on Next trial to start the next sequence.

The experiment includes only six trials. For each trial click on the word buttons that were in the sequence just presented.

When the experiment finishes, a new window will appear that reports on three measures. First, it will report the percentage of times that you correctly selected an item that was in the sequence. Second, it will report the percentage of times that you (incorrectly) selected a distractor not presented, but not the special distractor. Third, it will report the percentage of times that you (incorrectly) selected the special distractor that was hypothesized to correspond to a false memory. You should find that the percentage of time you select the special distractor is larger than the percentage for other distractors and is smaller than the percentage for correct selections.

Results of this type can occur for more complex and meaningful memories as well. Loftus (1993) describes implanting a false memory in a teenager. With her method, the teenager developed a memory of being lost in a mall when he was five years old. After the initial implant, the teenager reported additional details of the event that were never suggested, and never happened. Research findings related to false memories should serve as a warning to therapists who try to recover "lost" memories. There is a danger that the therapist may implant a false memory rather than find a lost one.

Additional References

Arndt, J. & Reder, L. M. (2003). The effect of distinctive visual information on false recognition. *Journal of Memory & Language, 48*(1), 1-15.

Carry, M., Manning, C., Loftus, E. & Sherman, S. J. (1996). Imagination inflation: Imagining a childhood event inflates confidence that it occurred. *Psychonomic Bulletin and Review, 3*(2), 208-214.

Kassin, S. M. & Kiechel, K. L. (1996). The social psychology of false confessions: compliance, internalization, and confabulation. *Psychological Science, 7*(3), 122-128.

Seamon, J.G., Goodkind, M. S., Dumey, A. D., Dick, E., Aufseeser, M. S., Strickland, S. E., Woulfin, J. R., & Fung, N.S. (2003). "If I didn't write it, why would I remember it?": Effects of encoding, attention, and practice on accurate and false memory. *Memory & Cognition, 31*, 445-457.

Basic Questions

1. What is the difference between special distractors and the regular distractors?

2. Which of the two types of distractors, related or not-related, should you select more often as falsely being present on the list of words to be remembered?

3. Everyone is talking about the new reality show on television where a university professor is locked in a school with 15 students and only one is coming out with an A, while others are kicked out of the classroom. Slowly every week, another student is failed by the teacher and asked to get out. Students are talking about what happened on the last show when they get into a heated debated about some events. Each person was positive that things happened the way they remembered it. How could you use this lab to explain what has happened?

4. You are helping out with your cousin's birthday party. The kids decide to play the secret game, where they all sit in a circle and someone starts a secret and whispers it in the next child's ear. This secret goes all the way around the circle until the last person has to say what the secret was. You start the secret and whisper to the kid sitting beside you, "When I can't sleep at night, I get Rudy, my teddy bear, out and he makes me feel better". The last person in the circle stands up and says, "If I am awake at night, I find Tooty, my stuffed animal and he helps me sleep." What has happened to your secret?

5. You are listening to one of your friends telling a story about a weekend trip that he just went on. You've already heard the story before, so you aren't really paying attention to her, but you notice that she has changed the story from when she told you earlier. Is she a liar?

Advanced Questions

1. Do you think there are any ways to protect ourselves from false memories?

2. Why is the False Memories CogLab found under the subheading of metamemory?

Discussion Questions

1. Discuss why we would need to have an accurate memory or else life would be difficult.

2. Discuss how the results of the False Memory CogLab help us to understand the limitations of our memory system.

Forgot it All Along

There has been much controversy over the issue of recovered memories (for an excellent overview, see the book edited by Conway, 1997). This is the apparent finding that people who enter psychotherapy suddenly recover memories of events that happened to them years ago, usually memories of sexual abuse. Schooler, Bendiksen and Ambadar (1997) use the term discovered rather than recovered memories because the latter implies that the memories are of real events whereas the former is neutral on whether the memory is of a real event or not.

Schooler et al. (1997) note that there are three independent claims being made when a person in therapy discovers a memory:

1. The event that is remembered is a real event
2. The event was forgotten for a period of time
3. The event is suddenly remembered

Schooler et al. point out that these three elements are independent. For example, the event could be real and the memory could be accurate, but there might not have been a period during which the person was unaware of the event. Each of these claims can in principle be empirically evaluated.

Schooler et al (1997) found 4 cases in which they can demonstrate objectively (1) the original event occurred, (2) there was a period of time during which the person did not remember the event, and (3) the memory was suddenly discovered. What this demonstrates is not that all discovered memories are of real events, but rather that in at least some cases, a person can experience an event, can fail to remember that event, and then later can recall the event.

For the memory theorist, what is most interesting is the finding that at the time of discovery, the person has the experience of currently remembering the event but also believing they had not previously remembered the event. One explanation of this failure by people to remember that they had remembered has been termed the "forgot-it-all-along" effect (Schooler et al., 1997). [The name is based on the "knew-it-all-along" effect in which subjects who were told of a particular outcome over estimated what they would have known.] The basic idea is that during the discovered memory experience, the person thinks about the episode in a different way.

This demo is a laboratory analog of this "forgot-it-all-along" effect that was devised by Arnold & Lindsay (2002). No one is claiming that this is exactly the same effect as when people say they had not remembered being abused earlier but now they do. Rather, it is a demonstration that people can forget that they had remembered.

There are three phases. In Phase I, you will see a list of word pairs, a cue and a target. In Phase II, you will receive a cued-recall test. Sometimes the cue will be the same as in Phase I, and sometimes it will be different. In Phase III, you will be given a memory judgment task: you will be asked whether you recalled a target in the Phase II test. You should remember that you recalled an item better when the context is the same and you should forget that you recalled an item when the context is different.

For registration information go to http://coglab.wadsworth.com.

Start Phase I by pressing the space bar. You will see a long list of word pairs, such as car-PORT. The first word (in lower case letters) is a cue, and the second word (in UPPERCASE LETTERS) is a target. When the list is over, you will be in Phase II.

Press the space bar to start each trial Phase II. In this phase, your task is to produce the target (the second word) when shown the cue (the first word). You will see something like car-P--T. Type in the letters to complete the target with the one that you saw on the original list. If you can't remember, guess by typing in any two letters. Press the space bar to see the next test item. After Phase II is over, you will enter Phase III.

In Phase III, you will be given another test. You will be shown a pair of items, such as car-PORT, and you will be asked whether you remember entering the UPPERCASE word as a response in Phase II. Press 'Y' to indicate that yes, you do remember entering that word in Phase II; press 'N' to indicate that no, you do not remember entering that word in Phase II.

There are 88 word pairs in Phase I, and 88 trials in Phase II and III.

Your performance on the cued-recall test should reflect the encoding specificity principle: You should do better when the context word at test (Phase II) is the same as during study (Phase I) than when it is different. Of more interest in this demo is the forgot it all along effect. When the context word presented during the memory judgment task (Phase III) was the same as during the cued-recall test (Phase II), you should have been more accurate in remembering that you remembered. In other words, you should have forgotten that you remembered the target word more often in the different context condition.

Additional References

Schacter, D. L., Norman, K. A., & Koutstaal, W. (1997). The recovered memory debate: A cognitive neuroscience perspective. In M. A. Conway (Ed.), *Recovered Memories and False Memories: Debates in Psychology* (pp. 63–99). Oxford: Oxford University Press.

Schooler, J.W., Bendiksen, M., Ambadar, Z. (1997) Taking the middle line: Can we accommodate both fabricated and recovered memories of sexual abuse? In M. Conway (Ed) *False and Recovered Memories*, (pp. 251-292) Oxford, England: Oxford University Press.

Basic Questions

1. In phase II of the lab, you had to fill in the missing 2 letters of the target word. What kind of specific type of memory is this _____. Then in phase III, you had to respond either yes or no for each word shown, as to whether you remembered the target word form phase II, which is what specific

type of memory _____. Of the two specific types of memory, which is usually easier to do (greater accuracy)?

2. Think back to Phase II and the amount of time it took to fill in the missing letters of the target word and then to Phase III to the amount of time it took to say yes or no for each word. Which words took the greater amount of time to respond to? (Think in terms of the cue word that was paired with the target word)

3. After getting your mark for your philosophy test, you learn that a majority of the class failed. Your professor tells you not to worry that he will give you a second test and you can take the better of the two grades. Your performance on the second test was even worse than the first. As you are looking through your test, you found that you got things right the first time, but then got them wrong on the second test. How does this compare to the lab you just did?

4. Your best friend comes to you in a panic and tells you about a guy who has been following her around campus all day trying to talk to her. As she is relaying her story, you suddenly have a flashback to your first year at the campus when some guy jumped out of the bushes at you when you were going to you car. Why do you think you had a flashback of this specific memory?

5. While going downtown with your roommate, you find yourselves driving over a long bridge with water far below. When you look out of the window and down at the water you suddenly experience a weird feeling followed by a wave of panic. You've never experienced a fear of heights or bridges before so you mention this to your brother. He proceeds to tell the story of when the two of you were young and he pushed you off a log that ran over a creek in your backyard and you couldn't swim. Luckily your father pulled you out before you could drown. How could your sudden feeling of panic be explained?

Advanced Questions

1. The "forgot it all along" cognitive effect is similar to the physiological "opponent-process" effect in drug tolerance. The opponent process occurs when your body learns what specific environment you tend to do drugs. Stimulants, like cocaine, puts the body in an imbalanced state, so it learns to counteract this affect before hand (hence the name opponent) by slowing down the heart. When you change environments, but still take high doses of cocaine (due to tolerance for the effect), the body isn't given a chance to counter the effects of it and overdoses are common. Discuss how this opponent process is similar to "forgot it all along"?

2. When people get into serious accidents that involve traumatic head injuries, they can have problems remembering what happened to them before the accident. How might this be comparable to the repressed memories from bad childhood experiences?

Discussion Questions

1. We depend on our memories for a number of reasons in our society. Discuss some of the problems that affect our memories. Start with the major problems that are discussed in this lab
2. and then think about other memory labs or information that you have learned from class. Be specific in your answers.

8.1 PROTOTYPES & EXEMPLARS

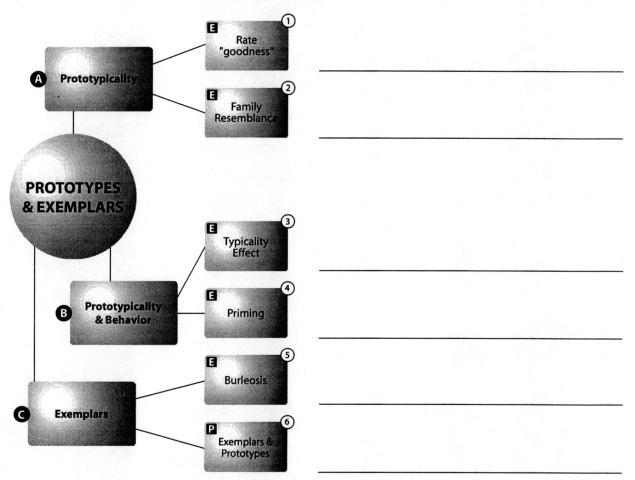

A What is prototypicality and how can it be demonstrated?

① **Experiment:** What is the result when people are asked to rate how "good" items are as representatives of a category? (Rosch; 271)

② **Experiment:** What is "family resemblance" and how is it related to prototypicality? (Rosch and Mervis; 272)

B How is prototypicality related to behavior?

③ **Experiment:** How was the sentence verification technique used to demonstrate the typicality effect? (Smith; 273)

④ **Experiment:** Describe the experiment that determined how priming is related to prototypicality. (Rosch; 274)

C What is the exemplar approach to categorization?

⑤ **Experiment:** What is the exemplar approach to categorization and how do the results of the burlosis experiment support this approach? (Medin; 277)

⑥ **Principle:** Which approach–prototypes or exemplars–best describes how people use categories? (278)

8.2 LEVELS OF CATEGORIES

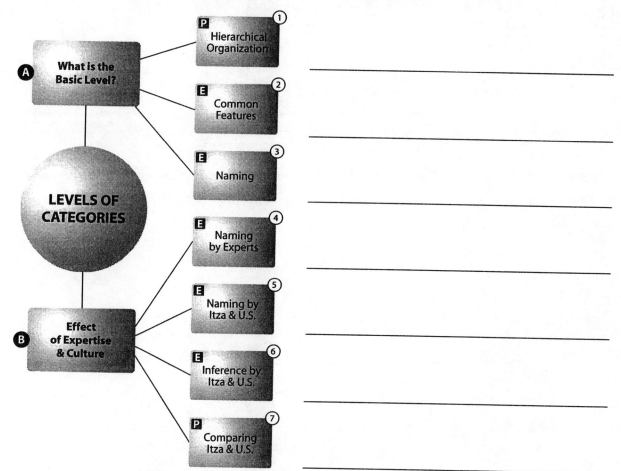

A **Is there a psychologically "privileged" level of categories?**

① **Principle:** What is the hierarchical organization of categories? What are the three levels of categories, according to Rosch? (279)

② **Experiment:** Describe the results of the experiment in which people listed common features for different levels of a category. How do the results support the idea that there is something special about Rosch's "basic" level? (Rosch; 280)

③ **Experiment:** Describe the results of (a) the experiment in which people named an object as quickly as possible; (b) the experiment in which people had to indicate whether an object was a member of a category. (Rosch; 281)

B **How do expertise and culture affect categorization?**

④ **Experiment:** How do bird experts and non-experts respond when asked to assign names to pictures of birds? (Tanaka & Taylor; 282)

⑤ **Experiment:** How do members of the Itza culture categorize plants and animals? How does this compare with the way U. S. college students categorize plants and animals? (Coley; 283)

⑥ **Experiment:** Describe the experiment in which Itza and U.S. participants were asked to make inferences about members of a category. (Coley; Medin & Atran; 283)

⑦ **Principle:** How is the categorization behavior of U. S. and Itza participants similar? How is it different? (284)

8.3 SEMANTIC NETWORK APPROACH

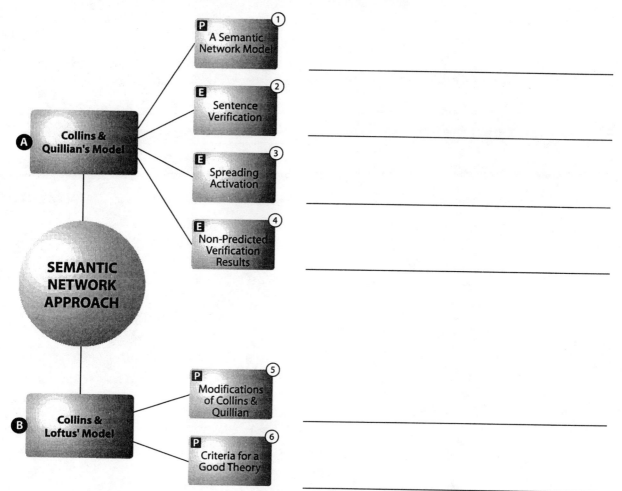

A   **What is the semantic network approach to concepts?**

① **Principle:** Describe Collins and Quillian's semantic network model. Be sure you understand the function of nodes and links and the idea of cognitive economy. (286)

② **Experiments:** Describe the results of the experiments using the sentence verification task that supported the Collins & Quillian model. (Collins & Quillian; 288)

③ **Experiment:** What is spreading activation? How do the results of the experiment that used the lexical decision task support the idea of spreading activation? (Meyer & Schvaneveldt; 289)

④ **Experiment:** Describe two situations in which the sentence verification task yielded results that were not predicated by the Collins and Quillian model. (Rips; 291)

B   **How was the Collins and Quillian model revised by Collins and Loftus?**

⑤ **Principle:** Describe the semantic network model proposed by Collins and Loftus. (292)

⑥ **Principle:** What are the properties of good psychological theories? Which of these properties do each of the semantic network models possess? (293)

8.4 CONNECTIONISM

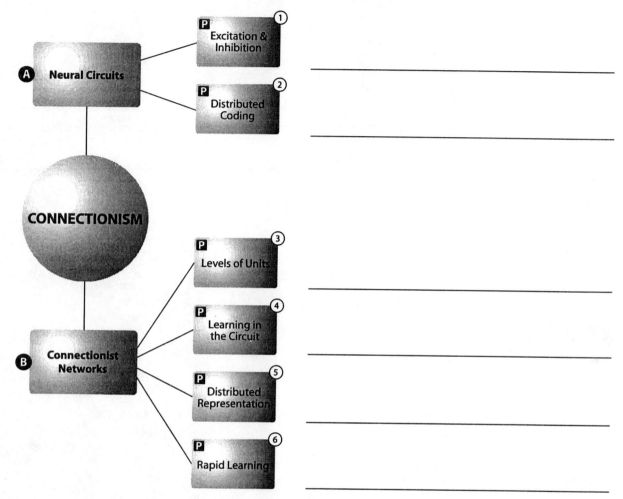

A **What are some basic facts about neural circuits that have been incorporated into connectionist theory?**

① **Principle:** Describe the way excitation and inhibition in neural circuits determines the rate at which a neuron will fire. (295)

② **Principle:** Describe the principle of distributed coding. (296)

B **What are the properties of connectionist networks?**

③ **Principle:** Describe the different levels of units (input, hidden and output) in a connectionist network. (297)

④ **Principle:** Describe how a connectionist network can "learn," so that a specific pattern of activity becomes associated with a specific concept. (298)

⑤ **Principle:** Where is knowledge about a concept contained in a connectionist network? How does this compare to the way knowledge is stored in a semantic network? (299)

⑥ **Principle:** What idea have connectionist researchers proposed to deal with the fact that people can learn some things very rapidly? (301)

8.5 CATEGORIES IN THE BRAIN

A How do the effects of brain damage provide evidence that specific areas of the brain are selective for categories?

① **Principle:** What is visual agnosia? (304)

② **Principle:** How do neuropsychological cases provide evidence for a double dissociation for living vs. non-living things? What does this mean? What case makes "things interesting"? (304)

B How do measurements of brain activity provide evidence that areas of the brain are selective for categories?

③ **Principle:** What do the results of fMRI research indicate about where tools and living things are represented in the brain? (304)

④ **Principle:** What are the characteristics of category-specific neurons? (304)

Prototypes

Part of cognitive psychology explores the concept of concepts. What cognitive events happen when you think about a chair? How is the concept of chair represented in the cognitive system? This is a subtle issue. For example, surely a seat at a formal dining table is chair, but what about a recliner, a stool, a couch, or a tree stump? The issue is important because the representation of concepts is the basis of everything else we can mentally do with concepts. In a very real sense how we think and what we can learn is largely determined by how we represent concepts.

An efficient way to represent concepts would be to keep only the critical properties of a concept. This set of critical properties is sometimes called a prototype or schema. The idea of prototypes is that a person has a mental construct that identifies typical characteristics of various categories. When a person encounters a new object he/she compares it to the prototypes in memory. If it matches the prototype for a chair well enough the new object will be classified and treated as a chair. This approach allows new objects to be interpreted on the basis of previously learned information. It is a powerful approach because one does not need to store all previously seen chairs in long term memory. Instead, only the prototype needs to be kept.

This experiment allows you to participate in a type of experiment that is often used to investigate the creation and storage of concepts. It is a variation of a method used by Posner and Keele (1968), which is one of the earliest studies to systematically explore concept representation in a controlled way. Rather than using an already well-known concept like a chair, Posner and Keele had participants learn patterns of dots. The patterns were variations of a few prototypes, but the prototypes themselves were not seen during a training phase. During the training phase participants learned to classify the variations, with the underlying prototype being the basis for correct classifications.

After learning to classify the variants, participants were shown a variety of dot patterns. In particular, they were shown patterns that were shown during the training phase, new variant patterns, and the patterns corresponding to the prototypes. Classification and reaction time performance were nearly equal for the previously seen variants and the prototypes. Performance was slightly worse for the new variants. This is significant because both the new variants and the prototypes were never seen during testing. To classify dot patterns that were not previously seen, the participants must be using a mental concept of what corresponds to the different categories. Since performance is better for the prototype patterns than for the new variants, the mental concept is similar to the prototype patterns. The conclusion seemed to be that people created a mental representation that was a mixture of the variant patterns used during training, that is, a prototype.

Posner and Keele's experiment led to an intense investigation on concept formation and representation. Much of that research is consistent with prototype theories. However, there are aspects of the experimental data (even in Posner and Keele's experiment) that suggest that the prototype theories cannot be the sole basis for concept representation. For example, our behavior is often influenced by the properties of individual experiences, and some theories of concept formation suggest that this alone can account for the data purported to imply prototypes. Nevertheless, prototypes are a part of many theories of cognition in a variety of forms. This demonstration is a variation of Posner and Keele's experiment.

After clicking on the experiment on the CD start page; use the drop down menu for instructions. Following are the instructions for Prototypes as seen on the CD.

Press the space bar to start a trial. A fixation point will appear for a second and then will be replaced by randomly placed dots. Your task is to classify the dot pattern as A (press the z-key) or as B (press the /-key [slash-key]). On the first few trials you may not properly classify the patterns, but you will receive feedback on each trial and so can learn which pattern corresponds to which keypress. You should make your responses as quickly as possible, but try to be accurate.

What follows are more detailed instructions.

After clicking on the experiment, a window will appear that fills the screen. Press the space bar to start a trial. After the bar press a fixation point will appear for a second and then will be replaced by randomly placed dots. Your task is to classify the dot pattern as z or as / by pressing those respective keys. On the first few trials you will not be able to properly classify the patterns, but you will receive feedback on each trial and so can learn which pattern corresponds to which keypress. You should make your responses as quickly as possible, but try to be accurate.

The experiment consists of separate training and testing phases. The training phase includes at least 60 trials (trials where a mistake is made are repeated later in the experiment) and the testing phase contains at least 30 trials. Each dot pattern in the training phase is a variation of one of two fixed prototype random dot patterns. The variations are made by randomly taking ten of the twenty-five dots in a prototype and moving them to a new position.

After completing the training phase, a new set of dot patterns is presented. The transition from training to testing is fairly seamless, and you might not notice when it happens. The dot patterns in the testing phase are of six types. One is the prototype that corresponds to the classification of z. Another is the prototype that corresponds to the classification of /. The other four patterns are new variations of these prototypes (two variations for each prototype). Each dot pattern is presented five times in random order.

Throughout this experiment your task is always the same. As quickly as possible classify the pattern as z or /. Press the space bar to start the next trial.

At the end of the experiment a new window will appear that reports the average reaction time (in milliseconds) to classification of the dot patterns in the testing phase. You should find that the reaction time to the prototype patterns is faster than the reaction time to the new variants.

Additional References

Blanton, H., Vanden Eijnden, R. J., Buunk, B. P., Gibbons, F. X., Gerrard, M. & Bakker, A. (2001). Negatively-framed and positively-framed prototypes in the prediction and prevention of unsafe sex. *Journal of Applied Social Psychology, 31*, 274 - 295.

Chown, E., Kaplan, S. & Kortenkamp, D. (1995) Prototypes, Location, and Associative Networks (PLAN): Towards a Unified Theory of Cognitive Mapping. *Cognitive Science, 19*, 1-51.

Koutstaal, W., Schacter, D. L., Verfaellie, M., Brenner, C. & Jackson, E. M. (1999).Perceptually-based false recognition of novel objects in amnesia: Effects of category size and similarity to category prototypes. *Journal of Cognitive Neuropsychology, 16*, 317-341.

Palmeri, T. J. & Nosofsky, R.. M. (2001). Central tendencies, extreme points, and prototype enhancement effects in ill-defined perceptual categorization. *The Quarterly Journal of Experimental Psychology, 54*, 197-235.

Basic Questions

1. What is a prototype? What is another name for prototype?

2. According to the prototype theory, how do we categorize new objects?

3. How would your results support a Prototype effect?

4. Your colleague is going to the deli across the street for lunch and asks if you want anything. You brought your lunch but you don't have any fruit, so you ask him to bring you back a piece of fruit. When your colleague comes back, he brings you this red thing he calls a pomegranate, a popular treat in his country, but something you have never experienced and have no idea how to eat. How could you explain the confusion?

Advanced Questions

1. How do you think items that fall on the fuzzy borders of a concept are handled?

2. How could categorization be defined as a social learning phenomenon?

Discussion Questions

1. Discuss the possibility that humans are not the only animals that categorize events or items in their environment.

2. Discuss the benefits and the drawbacks to categorizing objects based on prototypes.

Lexical Decision

Theories of human language propose that there exists a mental dictionary, a lexicon, which contains a variety of information about words. This lexicon contains information about a word's meaning (its semantic content), its part of language (noun, verb, adjective), and its relationships to other words (what can it follow?, what can follow it?, how can it be modified?). Psychologists are interested in the organization of this lexicon.

The lexicon is similar to a dictionary in that it holds information about words and other components of language. Physical dictionaries generally organize words alphabetically. This arrangement makes it easy to find any word, provided the spelling is known (or can be guessed). Because dictionaries are usually used to find the meanings of known words (or to check if a word is spelled properly), this organization is useful.

In the mental lexicon, though, the most useful feature of a word may not be its spelling, but its meaning, and its relationship to other words. If words are arranged in the lexicon by semantic relationships, then words that are related to each other (e.g., chair, seat, table,...) would be close in the lexicon, while words that are unrelated to each other (e.g., chair, dinosaur, broccoli,...) would be far apart.

Meyer and Schvaneveldt (1971) tested theories of this type using a lexical decision task. Words and pseudowords (e.g., "blar", or "plome") are presented and observers determine, as quickly as possible, whether or not the presented item is a valid word. Determining whether the item is a word involves searching the lexicon to see if the item is present. The time needed to make a "word" response indicates the time needed to search the lexicon to find the target word.

Meyer and Schvaneveldt hypothesized that search time would be shorter if the previously searched for word was close to the current target word. Search time would be longer if two successive words were in very different places in the lexicon. To test this hypothesis they presented pairs of items in sequence, and asked observers to judge each item in the pair as a word or nonword. They expected that the reaction time to the second item would be fastest if it was a word and the first item in the pair was a word that was semantically associated to the second item. The data showed exactly this effect.

You can find a similar effect searching through a physical dictionary, but with alphabetical order playing the important role. It will take less time to find the word "salivate" after searching for "salamander" and more time to find "salivate" after searching for "boomerang".

This experimental result has been taken as strong evidence for a class of theories based on spreading activation. These theories hypothesize that recognizing or thinking of a word involves activation of a node that codes that word. This activation spreads to nearby (semantically related) nodes, thereby priming those nodes and allowing faster response times in the lexical decision task. By running this type of task for many different types of words, one could, in theory, generate a description of semantic organization of the lexicon.

178

The results of this experiment are interesting for more than academic reasons. Many theories of language development and memory are based on spreading activation theories, and those theories have been used to motivate different treatments for a variety of learning problems.

For registration information go to http://coglab.wadsworth.com.

After clicking on the start button, a window will fill the entire screen. Press the space bar to start a trial. After pressing the space bar, the screen will go dark and a small fixation square will appear in the middle of the screen. Fixate this square. Two to three seconds later, a word or nonword will appear above the fixation square. Decide if the item is a word or a nonword as quickly as possible. Press the / key if the item is a word. Press the z key if the item is not a word. The fixation square will turn red when you press either of these keys, so you will know your response has been recorded.

After making your decision, press the space bar. Two to three seconds later, a word or nonword will appear below the fixation square. Again, decide if the item is a word or nonword by pressing the z or / key as quickly as possible. You will receive feedback on whether you chose correctly.

After deciding on the item below the fixation square, press the space bar to start the next trial. There are at least 70 total trials. You must classify the items correctly for the trial to count, so if you find that you are making many classification mistakes, slow down. You can take a break after pressing the z or / key for the item below the fixation square; but do not press the space bar before taking the break. Pressing the t key will discard a trial (e.g., you sneeze or are otherwise interrupted). Discarded trials will be repeated later.

At the end of the experiment a window will appear that reports the reaction time to the second item for each of five cases. In the Associated case, both the first and second items are words, and the words are semantically related to each other. In the Unassociated case, both the first and second items are words, but they are not directly related to each other. In the other conditions one or both of the items is a nonword. You should find that reaction time is shorter for the Associated than the Unassociated case.

Additional References

Elbro, C., Borstrøm, I. & Petersen, D. K. (1998). Predicting dyslexia from kindergarten. The importance of distinctness of phonological representations of lexical items. *Reading Research Quarterly, 33*(1), 36-60.

Lukatela, G., & Turvey, M. T. (1991). Phonological access of the lexicon: Evidence from associative priming with pseudohomophones. *Journal of Experimental Psychology: Human Perception and Performance, 17,* 951-966.

Merikle, P. M. & Reingold, E. M. (1990). Recognition and lexical decision without detection: Unconscious perception? *Journal of Experimental Psychology: Human Perception and Performance, 16,* 574-583.

Napps, S. E. (1989).Morphemic relationships in the lexicon: Are they distinct from semantic and formal relationships? *Memory and Cognition, 17,* 729-739.

Shiffrin, R. M., Wagenmakers, E., & Zeelenberg, R. (2004). Non-word repetition priming in lexical decision reverses as a function of study task and speed stress. *Journal of Experimental Psychology: Learning, Memory, and Cognition, 30,* 270-277.

Basic Questions

1. What kind of information does a lexicon contain?

2. What should the results be for the Lexical Decision task?

3. What is the difference between the associated and the unassociated case?

4. How might priming be related to activation strength?

Advanced Questions

1. How could you use what you know about priming to give advice to people teaching children how to read?

2. How could the Lexical Decision task be used to test attentional processes in depressed patients?

Discsussion Questions

1. Discuss how Lexical Decision tasks support a connectionist model.

2. Discuss some potential problems that bilingual individuals might have with the storage and processing of lexical information.

Absolute Identification

Lots of research in cognitive psychology has focused on whether there is a fundamental limit on people's capacity to process information and, if so, what that limit is. It might often seem that we have almost unlimited potential, especially when it comes to identifying and recognizing different items. Think of all the different people you can identify, or cars, or animals, or buildings, or pieces of furniture. Given the ease with which all of these items can be identified, it comes as a surprise to most people to find that when items vary in just one dimension, they cannot identify even seven items. The research that demonstrates this limitation is often done using a procedure known as absolute identification.

In a typical absolute identification experiment, people are exposed to a set of stimuli that vary systematically along only one dimension (e.g. nine tones of different frequencies, or eight lines of different lengths). A label, often a digit, is associated with each stimulus. The task is simply to produce the correct label in response to the presentation of an item from the set.

When the items are evenly spaced, the first and last items in the series are identified most easily. In contrast, identification of the middle items is usually quite poor. Such effects are found for many dimensions, such as frequency, loudness, weight, area, line length, and semantic continua.

One curious aspect is that performance seems fundamentally limited: no matter how many trials you get, you never get perfect at this task as long as the stimuli vary along only one dimension (Shiffrin & Nosofsky, 1994). If the stimuli varied along two or more dimensions, the task becomes trivially easy. For example, you probably have no trouble identifying the letters in the alphabet.

This is because the letters vary on multiple dimensions including height (the letter 't' is taller than the letter 'e'), curvature (the letter 'i' is straight, the letter 's' is all curves), and others.

For registration information go to http://coglab.wadsworth.com.

Press the space bar to start a trial. On each trial a line is presented in the middle of the screen. Your task is to press a key that indicates which line you think it is. For example, if you think it is Line 2, press the 2 key. If you think it is Line 6, press the 6 key. The computer will tell if you were correct. If you were not correct, the computer will also tell which line it was.

On the first trial you will be shown each of the lines. This lets you see each type of line. There are 70 trials, which sounds like a lot, but it takes only a couple of seconds per trial.

When the experiment finishes, a new window will appear that shows you how well you identified each line length. For example, to see the number of times Line Length 3 was identified as Line Length 5, find 'Line 3', in the first column, and 'Line 5' in the first row, and then find the number where the row and column intersect. You should find that performance is worse for the middle item (Line 4) and is better as you get nearer the end stimuli. Furthermore, you should find that when you make a mistake, you are most likely to select an item very close to the correct item.

Additional References

Lacouture, Y. (1997). Bow, range and sequential effects in absolute identification: A response-time analysis. *Psychological Research, 60,* 121-123.

Harbensak, G, (1992). The consistency model: A process model for absolute judgment. *Journal of Experimental Psychology: Human Perception and Performance, 18,* 303-309.

Miller, G. A. (1956). The magical number seven plus or minus two: Some limits on our capacity for processing information. *Psychological Review, 63,* 81-97.

Rouder, J. (2001). Absolute identification with simple and complex stimuli. *Psychological Science, 12* (4). 318-322.

Siegel, J. A. & Siegel, W. (1977). Absolute identification of notes and intervals by musicians. *Perception and Psychophysics, 21,* 143-152.

Basic Questions

1. Would it make sense if the class results revealed that a majority of misidentification errors were found between line 4 and 5? Explain your answer.

2. Would the line identification task have been easier if the lines varied on length and thickness, where line 7 would have been the thickest and line 1 was the thinnest?

3. You are watching your favorite gardening show and the host is talking about making your own wedding flower arrangements. All of the flowers she is using are pink with varying bloom sizes. When the flower arrangement is completed, your roommate walks in and starts watching the program with you. She asks for the name of one particular flower and you say that it is one of three possibilities, but you are not absolutely sure which one it is. How could you explain your inability to determine exactly which of the three flowers it was?

4. You are new to campus and you're trying to find your way around, although you are having trouble finding the psychology building. You stop a passing student and ask them if they know where Vari Hall is (psychology is housed in this building). They point over your shoulder to the right and tell you it is the tall building and walk away quickly. When you look in the pointed direction you see 5 identical buildings, but 3 look to be taller than the other 2. Why will you have trouble identifying Vari Hall?

5. In a study that you are doing, you have to taste 7 dark brown fluids and rank them from 1-7 for their sweetness, with 7 being the sweetest and 1 being not at all sweet. After tasting all 7, you start to rank them, immediately setting fluid C in position 1 and fluid F in position 7. Why do you think these preference positions were the easiest to determine? Which positions might be the hardest to rank? Why?

Advanced Questions

1. For your summer break, you decide to travel to South Africa to volunteer in a remote village. The males of this tribe look identical except for a decorative bone they wear in their nose lengthways. You are told that the length of the bone correlates with the man's status, so the longer the bone the greater the status. It is important that you learn each man's status within the tribe so you can greet him accordingly. What kind of problems could you encounter with this task?

2. For Christmas, your mother bought you a clock that chimes like a tugboat on the hour. At 12:00, the tugboat toots goes on for 24 seconds and at 1:00 the chimes last for 2 seconds. If you were trying to tell the time by the tooting, what kinds of problems could you face? Give specific examples of potential problems.

3. Come up with an Absolute Identification example, using the volume range on a stereo system from 1-10, with 1 being the lowest and 10 being the loudest setting. In this example, describe the problems with absolute identification of volume level, as well as the conditions that need to apply for this phenomenon to be considered. Be creative.

Discussion Questions

1. Discuss how the results of this lab contribute to the idea that humans have a limited capacity for processing information.

2. The concept of Absolute Identification has been applied to cross-cultural errors in identifying people. For example, errors increase when a Caucasian tries to identify a Chinese person. Discuss how the increased errors could be explained.

9.1 IMAGERY IN THE HISTORY OF PSYCHOLOGY

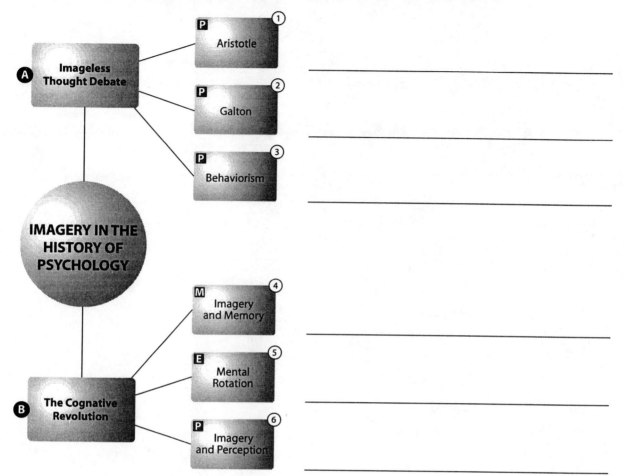

A **What was the imageless thought debate?**

① **Principle:** What was Aristotle's idea about the connection between imagery and thought? (312)

② **Principle:** What evidence did Galton cite as an argument against the idea that imagery always accompanies thought? (312)

③ **Principle:** How did behaviorism affect research on imagery? (312)

B **How was imagery research "reborn" during the cognitive revolution?**

④ **Method:** How did Paivio determine a link between imagery and memory? (313)

⑤ **Experiment:** Describe the experiment that demonstrated mental rotation. Why was this experiment important? (Shepard & Metzler; 313)

⑥ **Principle:** What is the basis for the idea that imagery and perception share the same mechanisms? (314)

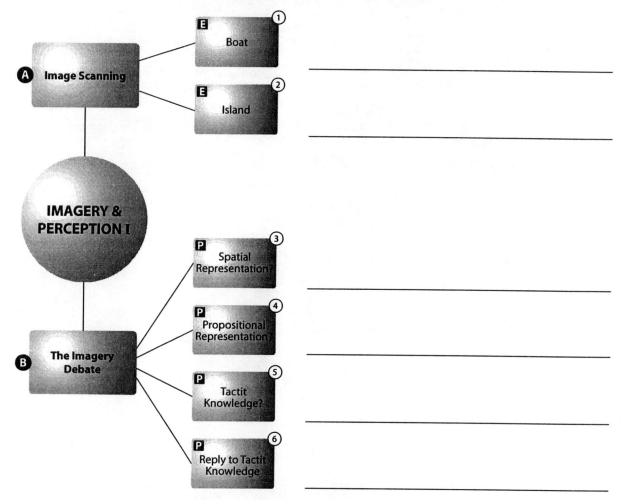

A **What were the results of the image scanning experiments?**

① **Experiment:** Describe the experiment in which participants scanned their mental image of a boat. How did Kosslyn interpret the results of this experiment? (Kosslyn; 315)

② **Experiment:** Describe the experiment in which participants scanned their mental image of locations on an island. (Kosslyn; 316)

B **What are the arguments in the "imagery debate"?**

③ **Principle:** Describe the "spatial" side of the imagery debate. (316)

④ **Principle:** Describe the "propositional" side of the imagery debate. When Pylyshyn said that imagery is an epiphenomenon, what did he mean? How can Kosslyn's boat and island experiments be represented propositionally? (318)

⑤ **Principle:** What is the tacit knowledge explanation of the results of the scanning experiments? (320)

⑥ **Experiment:** Describe the experiment that was done to answer the tacit knowledge explanation of the scanning experiments. (Finke & Pinker; 320)

9.3 IMAGERY & PERCEPTION II

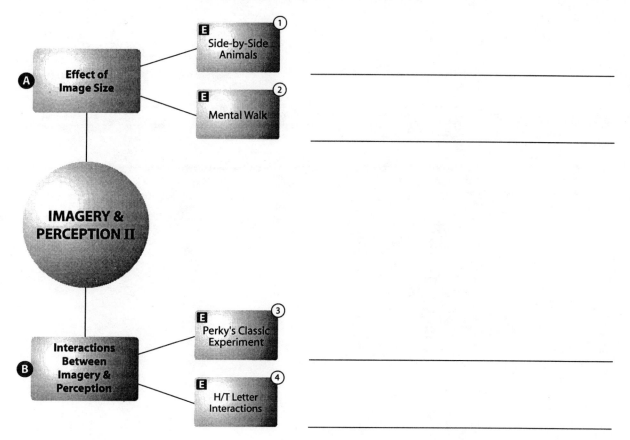

A **What occurs when the size of a mental image is changed?**

① **Experiment:** Describe the experiment in which participants were asked to imagine large and small animals next to each other. (Kosslyn; 321)

② **Experiment:** Describe the results of the experiment that used the "mental walk task". What did Kosslyn conclude from the results of this experiment? (Kosslyn; 321)

B **How do imagery and perception interact?**

③ **Experiment:** Describe the experiment in which participants "projected" visual images onto a screen. (Perky; 323)

④ **Experiment:** Describe the experiment in which participants imaged the letter "H" or "T" on a screen and then did a perceptual task. (Farah; 323)

9.4 IMAGERY & THE BRAIN

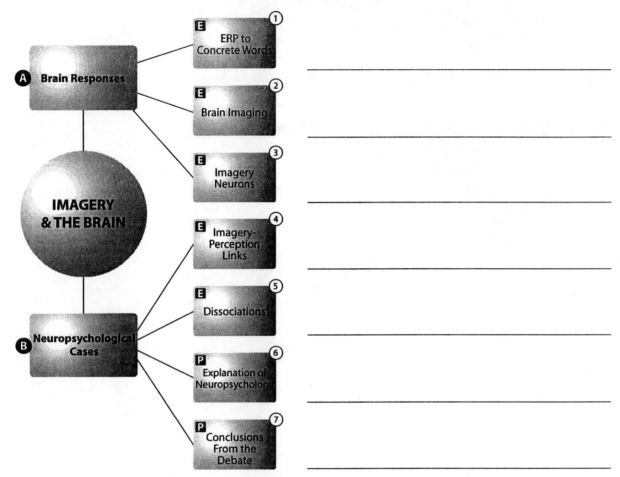

(A) **How can measuring the way the brain responds to imagery help resolve the imagery debate?**

(1) **Experiment:** Describe the experiment that measured the ERP elicited by concrete nouns and abstract nouns. (Farah; 326)

(2) **Experiments:** What evidence supports the idea that imagery creates a response in area V1? (LiBihan; Goldenberg; Kosslyn; 327)

(3) **Experiment:** Describe imagery neurons. What distinguishes an imagery neuron from a category-specific neuron? (Kreiman; 328)

(B) **What do studies of people with brain damage tell us about the nature of imagery?**

(4) **Experiments (Neuropsychology):** Describe the correspondence between imagery and perception that was demonstrated (a) by removal of M.G.S.'s poccipital lobe (Farah; 329); (b) by testing a patient with unilateral neglect. (Bisiach & Luzzatti; 331)

(5) **Experiments (Neuropsychology):** What two kinds of dissociations between imagery and perception have been observed? (Various researchers; 332)

(6) **Principle:** What "paradox" is presented by the neuropsychological cases? How has this paradox been explained in terms of bottom-up and top-down processing? (332)

(7) **Principle:** What can we conclude about the imagery debate? (335)

9.5 IMAGERY & MEMORY

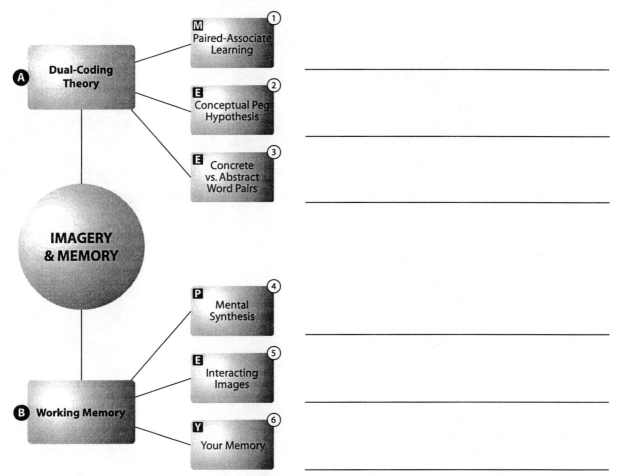

A **What is dual-coding theory?**

① **Method:** How would you run a paired-associate learning experiment? (336)

② **Experiment:** What is dual-coding theory? What result led Paivio to propose the conceptual peg hypothesis, and what is that hypothesis? (Paivio; 336)

③ **Experiment:** How was it shown that concrete adjective-noun pairs are remembered better than abstract pairs? How does this result support the conceptual peg hypothesis? (Begg; 337)

B **How has the original working memory model described in Chapter 5 (see page 162) been updated?**

④ **Principle:** What is mental synthesis and how has the process of mental synthesis been described by the updated model of working memory? (338)

⑤ **Experiment:** How do interactions between images, and the bizarreness of images affect memory? (Wollen; 339)

⑥ **Your Experience:** Pick something you need to do later today and create an image that will help you remember what you need to do.

Mental Rotation

When we carry out some cognitive tasks we seem to use mental images. For example, how many windows are in your house or apartment? To answer this question most people seem to recall a mental map of their apartment and, mentally, move through the map as they count windows.

Although everyone seems to experience something that we call mental imagery, it is difficult to draw conclusions from such introspections. For example, some people report that their mental images are very sketchy and ill defined, while others report their mental images are detailed and crisp. Based solely on these reports, it is impossible to know whether people's mental images really differ, or if some subjects just describe the mental images differently.

To explore mental images more objectively, researchers give subjects tasks that seem to require the use of mental images. As a critical part of the task is varied, some characteristics of mental images can be deduced. Roger Shepard and his colleagues (e.g., Shepard & Metzler, 1971) designed one of the most often used tasks. In this task subjects were shown two novel visual stimuli and were asked to determine whether the stimuli had the same shape or different shapes. The shapes (random block shapes) were rotated either in the plane or in depth. Subjects reported that they mentally rotated an image in their head until the two stimuli were oriented the same way, and then made their judgment.

When subjects were asked to make their response as quickly as possible, the reaction time increased with the angle of rotation between the shapes. This suggests that it takes time to mentally rotate an image, and implies that mental images are much like real images. Shepard further found that every 50 degrees of physical rotation required one second of mental rotation before subjects could respond. This suggests that the rate of mental rotation is at a constant velocity.

Shepard's findings have had a large influence on theories of mental representation. This experiment allows you to participate in a variation of the mental rotation task.

For registration information go to http://coglab.wadsworth.com.

Start a trial by pressing the space bar. Two random shapes will appear on the screen, one to the left and one to the right. The two shapes are either identical, or one is a mirror image of the other. One shape is also rotated clockwise 0, 45, 90, or 135 degrees relative to the orientation of the other shape. Your task is to determine whether the two shapes are mirror images or not. Respond as quickly as possible by pressing the z key (for "mirror") or the / key (for "not mirror"). You will receive feedback on whether you were correct. When you are ready for the next trial, press the space bar again.

There is a minimum of 80 trials. For each "mirror" and "not mirror" condition 10 trials are presented for each rotation angle. If you make a mistake (e.g., say the stimuli are mirrors when they were not), the trial will be repeated (with different stimuli) later in the experiment. In this way, only reaction times where you were correct are used. If you find you are often making mistakes, you should try slowing down on your responses and/or try harder.

When you finish the experiment a window will appear that plots reaction time as a function of rotation angle, with separate curves for "Mirror" and "Same" trials. You should find that both curves increase with rotation angle, and that the curves are nearly straight lines.

Additional References

Brosnan, M. J. (1998). Spatial ability in children's play with Lego blocks. Perceptual and Motor Skills, 87, 19-28.

Delgado, A. R. & Prieto, G. (1996). Sex differences in visuospatial ability: Do performance factors play such an important role? *Memory & Cognition, 24*, 504-510.

De Lisi, M. & Wolford., J. L. (2002). Improving children's mental rotation accuracy with computer game playing. *Journal of Genetic Psychology, 163* (3) 272-283.

Levine, S. C., Huttenlocher, J., Taylor, A., & Langrock, A. (1999). Early sex differences in spatial skill. *Developmental Psychology, 35*, 940-949.

Linn, M. C. & Petersen, A. C. (1985). Emergence and characterization of gender differences in spatial abilities: A meta-analysis. *Child Development, 56*, 1479-1498.

Masters, M. S. & Sanders, B. (1993). Is the gender difference in mental rotation disappearing? *Behavior Genetics, 23*, 337-341.

Basic Questions

1. When you were doing the lab, which of the four degree rotations did you have to spend more time thinking about in order to get the correct answer? Which degree rotation took you the shortest time to think about?

2. Are the diagrams in this experiment two dimensional or three dimensional? Which specific dimensions do the shapes have?

3. Your sister is taking a Tai Chi class at school, but she is having a lot of problems copying the different moves from the instructor. You ask her if the instructor faces her or has her back to the students. Why might this make a difference?

4. You are bored of studying and decide to go visit your grandmother. On your way to her house, you have to detour because of construction and you end up on the other side of her subdivision. As you try to find her house, you drive right past her house, not recognizing it until you pass by. Why do you think you didn't recognize it?

5. You are trying to teach your little sister how to make different designs by transferring string from one person's hands to the others. You notice that she has to walk around you to recognize the shape

that you've created. She usually recognizes what to do when she is standing beside you. How can you explain what she is doing now that you have done this lab?

Advanced Questions

1. How do you think an individual who in fluent in the American Sign Language (ASL) might perform on this mental rotation task and why?

2. Why do the results of the mental rotation experiments support the analog coding approach of mental images?

3. Shepard, one of the researchers who designed this experiment found that every 50 degrees of physical rotation required one second of mental rotation before subjects could respond. This suggests that the rate of mental rotation is at a constant velocity. What would the graph look like for this of data?

Discussion Questions

1. Discuss how a parent could improve their child's spatial ability by their selection of toys and games their child is exposed to. See the references provided for a clue.

2. How do you think older adults would perform on a Mental Rotation Task compared to younger adults? Explain your answer.

10.1 INTRODUCTION TO LANGUAGE

A Why can we say that language is *creative* and *universal*?

① **Principle:** What two properties of human language enable people to go far beyond the fixed calls and signals of animals? (346)

② **Principle:** What evidence supports the idea that language is "universal"? (346)

B How has language been studied?

③ **Principle:** What are aphasias? What two brain areas are associated with aphasia? (347)

④ **Principle:** Compare the way Skinner and Chomsky described language learning. (348)

⑤ **Principle:** What is psycholinguistics? (348)

10.2 UNDERSTANDING WORDS

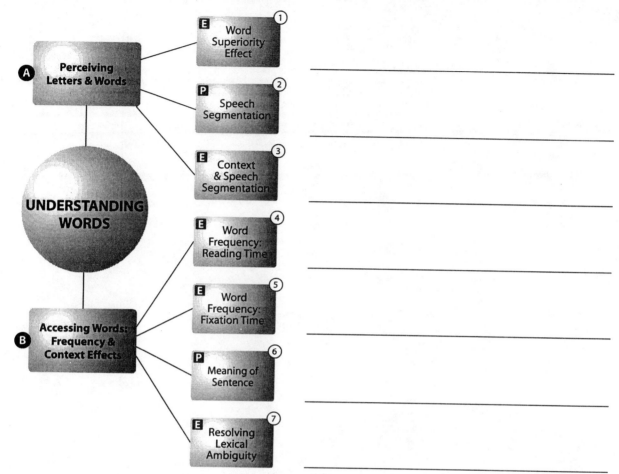

A **What processes are involved in the perception of letters and words?**

① **Experiment:** What is the word superiority effect and how was it demonstrated? (Wheeler; Reicher; 350)
② **Principle:** What is speech segmentation? What makes it difficult? (352)
③ **Experiment:** Describe the experiment in which participants were asked to identify words taken out of context. (Pollack & Pickett; 352) What kinds of information helps us solve the problem of speech segmentation? (352)

B **How do we understand words?**

④ **Experiment:** How was the lexical decision task used to demonstrate the word frequency effect? (Savin; 353)
⑤ **Experiment:** How have eye movement studies been used to demonstrate the word frequency effect? (Rayner; 354)
⑥ **Principle:** How does the way a word fits the meaning of a sentence affect how long it takes to understand the word? (355)
⑦ **Experiment:** What is lexical ambiguity? Describe the experiment that investigated how rapidly people resolve lexical ambiguity as they are reading a sentence. (Swinney; 355)

10.3 UNDERSTANDING SENTENCES I

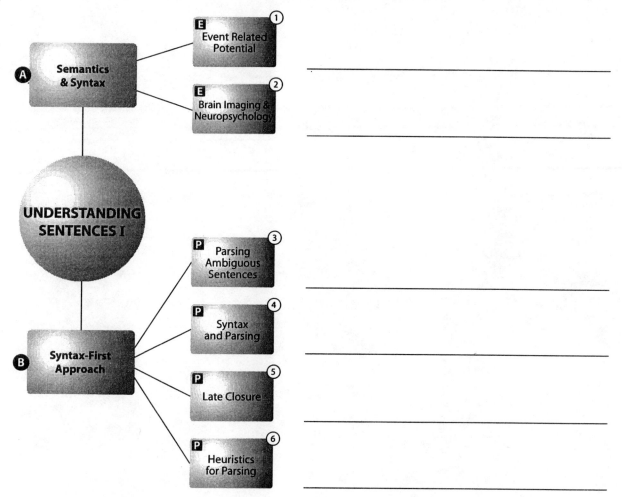

A How can we distinguish between semantics and syntax?

① **Experiment:** How are the N400 and N600 components of the ERP affected by semantics and syntax? (Osterhout; 358)

② **Experiments:** What do brain imaging and neuropsychological studies indicate about the representation of semantics and syntax in the brain? (Dapritte; Breedin; 359)

B What is the syntax-first approach to sentence understanding?

③ **Principle:** What is syntactic ambiguity and how is it related to the way a sentence is parsed? (359)

④ **Principle:** What does the selection from *Alice Through the Looking Glass* indicate about the connection between syntax and sentence understanding? (359)

⑤ **Principle:** What is the principle of late closure? Why is the syntax-first approach to sentence understanding also called the garden-path model? (360)

⑥ **Principle:** Why can the rule of late closure be called a "heuristic"?

10.4 UNDERSTANDING SENTENCES II

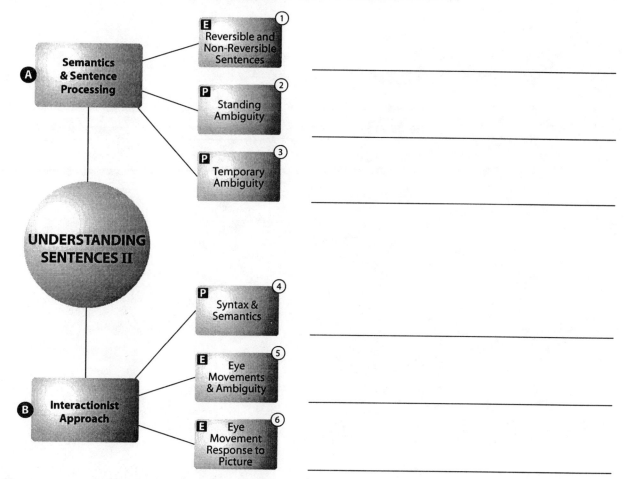

A **How can semantics influence sentence processing?**

① **Experiment:** Describe the experiment that demonstrated that non-reversible sentences can be understood more rapidly than reversible sentences. (Slobin; 362)

② **Principle:** What is standing ambiguity and how does it demonstrate the role of semantics in understanding sentences? (364)

③ **Principle:** What is temporary ambiguity and how does it demonstrate the role of semantics in understanding sentences? (364)

B **What is the interactionist approach to parsing?**

④ **Principle:** What does the interactionist approach propose regarding the order in which syntax and semantics are taken into account as a person reads a sentence? (365)

⑤ **Experiment:** Describe the experiment that measured eye movements as a person read sentences about a defendant, evidence, and a lawyer. What do the results of this experiment indicate about how the meaning of words in a sentence affects parsing? (Trueswell; 365)

⑥ **Experiment:** Describe the experiment that measured eye movements as a person heard a story about an apple while viewing a picture. (Tannehaus; 365)

10.5 UNDERSTANDING TEXT

 How do readers create connections between parts of a text?

① **Principle:** What is coherence? How is coherence related to inference? What are three different types of inference? (369)

② **Experiment:** Describe the experiment that used pairs of sentences about Jimmy's bruises, to investigate the relationship between coherence and memory. (Myers & Duffy; 372)

③ **Experiment:** What is a local connection? A global connection? Describe the experiment that used a paragraph about Mary ordering food, to investigate how global coherence affects reading time. (Albrecht & O'Brien; 373)

④ **Your experience:** Think about some movies you have seen recently in terms of how easy it was to make sense of the movie as you were viewing it. Can you draw a connection between "coherence" and "ease of understanding" in these movies?

B **What is a situation model for text understanding?**

⑤ **Experiment:** Describe the experiment in which participants had to indicate whether an object was in the same room as a man who was walking through a research center. (Morrow; 374)

⑥ **Experiment:** Describe the experiment in which a passage about the opening of an art gallery was used to investigate how readers process information about time in a story. How do the results of this experiment and the one in 5, above, relate to the idea of situation models? (Zwaan; 375)

10.6 UNDERSTANDING CONVERSATIONS

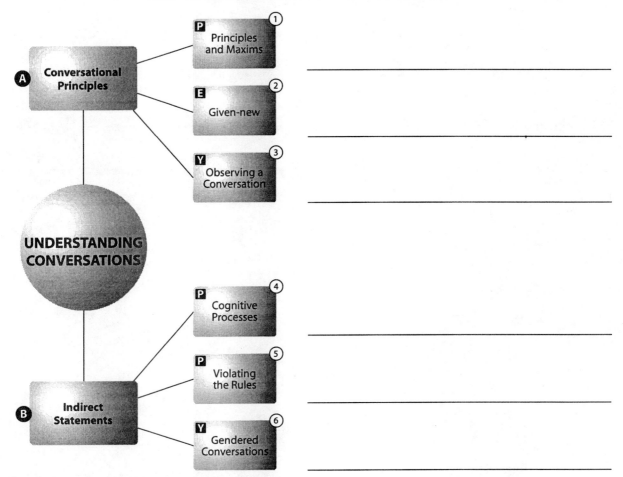

A **What are the basic principles of conversation?**

① **Principle:** What is Grice's conversational principle and his conversational maxims? (377)

② **Experiment:** Describe the experiment that used a sentence about checking picnic supplies to investigate the given-new contract. (Haviland & Clark; 378)

③ **Your Experience:** The next time you are having a conversation, be aware of how you and the other person are following (or not following) the basic principles of conversation.

B **How do people understand indirect statements?**

④ **Principle:** What kind of cognitive processes are involved in understanding indirect statements? (379)

⑤ **Principle:** What kinds of information can be provided by violations of conversational rules? (379)

⑥ **Your Experience:** Can you decide, based on your experience, whether there is a difference in the use of indirect statements by males and females?

10.7 CULTURE & LANGUAGE

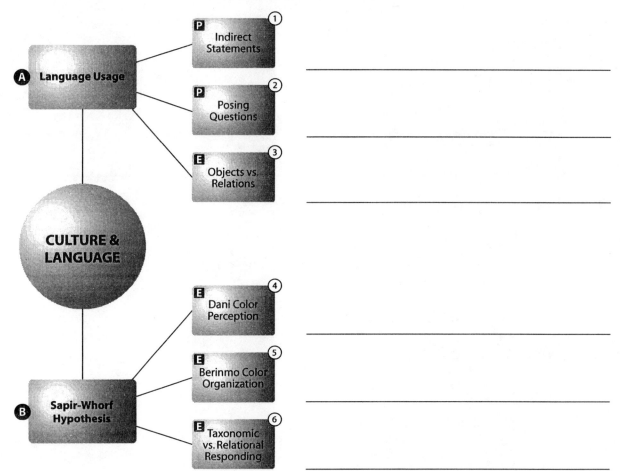

A Are there differences in how people from different cultures use language?

① **Principle:** Compare the use of indirect statements by Americans and East Asians. (380)

② **Principle:** Compare the way American speakers and Chinese speakers pose questions. What do these differences indicate? (380)

③ **Experiment:** Describe the experiment that determined how Japanese and American mothers talked with their 6-19-month-old children. (Fernald & Morikawa; 380)

B What is the evidence for a connection between language and thought (the Sapir-Whorf hypothesis)?

④ **Experiment:** What is the Sapir-Whorf hypothesis and how was it tested by comparing color perception and memory in Americans and the Dani? (Heider; 381)

⑤ **Experiment:** Describe the color naming and categorical perception experiments that were carried out on Berinmo and British participants. What do the results indicate about the Sapir-Whorf hypothesis? (Roberson; 381)

⑥ **Experiments:** Describe the experiments that compared how Americans and Chinese pair objects. What can we conclude about which cultures sort taxonomically and which sort relationally? (Chiu; Ji; 382)

Word Superiority

Humans are miraculously good at recognizing visual patterns. Even the fastest of modern computers are nowhere near as efficient or thorough at identifying visual targets. How we acquired this level of sophistication is not fully understood. What is clear is that context plays an important role in interpreting a physical stimulus. We are not simply detectors of patterns of light; instead we infer interpretations of the physical stimulus.

The effect of context is made clear in a phenomenon called the word superiority effect (Reicher, 1969). In the experiment an isolated letter like K or a word like WORK is briefly flashed on a screen and then immediately replaced by a mask of X's and O's. The observer is then forced to choose between whether a D or a K was presented. A key component of the experiment is that either of the choices at the end of WOR would create a valid word. Thus, the observer's knowledge that the presentation contained a word does not automatically tell him which letter was presented. Even with this control, the experimental finding is that detection of K is better when it is part of a word than when it is presented in isolation. This is the word superiority effect.

This result seems paradoxical. In detecting an isolated letter, there is only one item to focus on. When a word is presented, more letters must be processed before the word can be detected. Thus, it would seem, detecting a letter in a word should be more difficult than detecting a letter in isolation. The data, however, demonstrates exactly the opposite effect.

This finding has been of significant interest to researchers that explore the processes involved in recognizing patterns. Although the word superiority effect has been a motivating result for a variety of theories, the effect has not been completely explained by any current theory. This demonstration allows you to participate in a version of the word superiority experiment.

For registration information go to http://coglab.wadsworth.com.

After clicking on the start button, a window will appear to start the experiment. Start a trial by pressing the space bar. A fixation dot will appear in the middle of the window, stare at it. One second later a word or an isolated letter will briefly flash on the screen. The duration of this word or letter is very brief (approximately 40 milliseconds), then the word/letter is replaced with a mask of X's and O's. Half a second later, instructions will appear on which position you are to report on. These instructions are of the form *--- S or M? This indicates that you are to report on whether the letter in the first position is an S or an M. An instruction like --*- E or L? indicates that you are to report on whether the letter in the third position was an E or a L. Simply type in the letter that you saw at the indicated position. You will not receive any feedback on whether your guess was correct. The letter you type, however, will be shown in red on the bottom half of the screen. This indicates that the computer has registered the key you pressed.

You may find that in some trials you have no idea what the queried letter was. In those cases, just guess one of the options. (You may find that on the isolated letter trials you see a letter but it is in a different

213

place than you are queried. Guessing that letter might be a good strategy because with these brief duration's, things sometimes seem to jump around.)

Press the space bar to start the next trial. If you wish, before pressing the space bar, but after identifying the letter, you can check how many trials remain for the current experiment with the Trials to go pull-down menu.

There are a total of 96 trials. There are 16 four letter words and 16 isolated letters in different locations. Each condition is repeated three times. If you respond before the probe appears, the trial will be repeated later.

At the end of the experiment a new window will appear that reports the percentages of correct detection's in the word trials and the isolated letter trials. You should find that the percentage is larger for the detection of a target letter in a word than in isolation. If you are truly guessing on each trial, then your percentages should be close to 50%.

Additional References

Chase, C. H. & Tallal, P. (1990). A developmental, interactive activation model of the word superiority effect. *Journal of Experimental Child Psychology, 49,* 448-487.

Haerich, P. & Carmack, H. C. (1992). Erotophobia, erotophilia, and the word superiority effect. *Bulletin of the Psychonomic Society, 30,* 466.

Krueger, L. E. (1992). The word-superiority effect and phonological recoding. *Memory & Cognition, 20,* 685-694.

Peressotti, F. & Job, R. (1993).Lack of word-superiority effect in processing letter features. *Bulletin of The Psychonomic Society, 31,* 433-436.

Peterzell, D. H., Sinclair, G. P., Healy, A. F. & Bourne, L. E., Jr. (1990). Identification of letters in the predesignated target paradigm: A word superiority effect for the common word the. *American Journal of Psychology, 103,* 299-315.

Basic Questions

1. What would your results be like if a word superiority effect was present?

2. What might a 50% detection rate suggest?

3. A "sentence superiority effect" has been demonstrated for words. What would this effect be?

4. You have saved up enough money to go to Daytona Beach with your friends for March break. With all of the snow that you get Michigan, the sun and the heat are welcome changes. While walking along the beach, a guy comes up to you and starts talking to you like he knows you, but you have no idea who he is. A group of guys come along behind him and you suddenly recognize them from your Psychology class, including the guy you are talking to. How can you explain what happened to your memory?

Advanced Questions

1. How might the word or sentence superiority effects help to explain other phenomenon that suggests memories may be coded semantically?

2. How could top-down processing help to explain the word superiority effect?

Discussion Questions

1. Discuss how the Word Superiority effect might change with age?

2. Discuss whether you would expect to find a Word Superiority effect if the letters were in mixed casing, like fAdE.

Lexical Decision

Theories of human language propose that there exists a mental dictionary, a lexicon, which contains a variety of information about words. This lexicon contains information about a word's meaning (its semantic content), its part of language (noun, verb, adjective), and its relationships to other words (what can it follow?, what can follow it?, how can it be modified?). Psychologists are interested in the organization of this lexicon.

The lexicon is similar to a dictionary in that it holds information about words and other components of language. Physical dictionaries generally organize words alphabetically. This arrangement makes it easy to find any word, provided the spelling is known (or can be guessed). Because dictionaries are usually used to find the meanings of known words (or to check if a word is spelled properly), this organization is useful.

In the mental lexicon, though, the most useful feature of a word may not be its spelling, but its meaning, and its relationship to other words. If words are arranged in the lexicon by semantic relationships, then words that are related to each other (e.g., chair, seat, table,...) would be close in the lexicon, while words that are unrelated to each other (e.g., chair, dinosaur, broccoli,...) would be far apart.

Meyer and Schvaneveldt (1971) tested theories of this type using a lexical decision task. Words and pseudowords (e.g., "blar", or "plome") are presented and observers determine, as quickly as possible, whether or not the presented item is a valid word. Determining whether the item is a word involves searching the lexicon to see if the item is present. The time needed to make a "word" response indicates the time needed to search the lexicon to find the target word.

Meyer and Schvaneveldt hypothesized that search time would be shorter if the previously searched for word was close to the current target word. Search time would be longer if two successive words were in very different places in the lexicon. To test this hypothesis they presented pairs of items in sequence, and asked observers to judge each item in the pair as a word or nonword. They expected that the reaction time to the second item would be fastest if it was a word and the first item in the pair was a word that was semantically associated to the second item. The data showed exactly this effect.

You can find a similar effect searching through a physical dictionary, but with alphabetical order playing the important role. It will take less time to find the word "salivate" after searching for "salamander" and more time to find "salivate" after searching for "boomerang".

This experimental result has been taken as strong evidence for a class of theories based on spreading activation. These theories hypothesize that recognizing or thinking of a word involves activation of a node that codes that word. This activation spreads to nearby (semantically related) nodes, thereby priming those nodes and allowing faster response times in the lexical decision task. By running this type of task for many different types of words, one could, in theory, generate a description of semantic organization of the lexicon.

216

The results of this experiment are interesting for more than academic reasons. Many theories of language development and memory are based on spreading activation theories, and those theories have been used to motivate different treatments for a variety of learning problems.

For registration information go to http://coglab.wadsworth.com.

After clicking on the start button, a window will fill the entire screen. Press the space bar to start a trial. After pressing the space bar, the screen will go dark and a small fixation square will appear in the middle of the screen. Fixate this square. Two to three seconds later, a word or nonword will appear above the fixation square. Decide if the item is a word or a nonword as quickly as possible. Press the / key if the item is a word. Press the z key if the item is not a word. The fixation square will turn red when you press either of these keys, so you will know your response has been recorded.

After making your decision, press the space bar. Two to three seconds later, a word or nonword will appear below the fixation square. Again, decide if the item is a word or nonword by pressing the z or / key as quickly as possible. You will receive feedback on whether you chose correctly.

After deciding on the item below the fixation square, press the space bar to start the next trial. There are at least 70 total trials. You must classify the items correctly for the trial to count, so if you find that you are making many classification mistakes, slow down. You can take a break after pressing the z or / key for the item below the fixation square; but do not press the space bar before taking the break. Pressing the t key will discard a trial (e.g., you sneeze or are otherwise interrupted). Discarded trials will be repeated later.

At the end of the experiment a window will appear that reports the reaction time to the second item for each of five cases. In the Associated case, both the first and second items are words, and the words are semantically related to each other. In the Unassociated case, both the first and second items are words, but they are not directly related to each other. In the other conditions one or both of the items is a nonword. You should find that reaction time is shorter for the Associated than the Unassociated case.

Additional References

Elbro, C., Borstrøm, I. & Petersen, D. K. (1998). Predicting dyslexia from kindergarten. The importance of distinctness of phonological representations of lexical items. *Reading Research Quarterly, 33*(1), 36-60.

Lukatela, G., & Turvey, M. T. (1991). Phonological access of the lexicon: Evidence from associative priming with pseudohomophones. *Journal of Experimental Psychology: Human Perception and Performance, 17,* 951-966.

Merikle, P. M. & Reingold, E. M. (1990). Recognition and lexical decision without detection: Unconscious perception? *Journal of Experimental Psychology: Human Perception and Performance, 16,* 574-583.

Napps, S. E. (1989).Morphemic relationships in the lexicon: Are they distinct from semantic and formal relationships? *Memory and Cognition, 17,* 729-739.

Shiffrin, R. M., Wagenmakers, E., & Zeelenberg, R. (2004). Non-word repetition priming in lexical decision reverses as a function of study task and speed stress. *Journal of Experimental Psychology: Learning, Memory, and Cognition, 30,* 270-277.

Basic Questions

1. What kind of information does a lexicon contain?

2. What should the results be for the Lexical Decision task?

3. What is the difference between the associated and the unassociated case?

4. How might priming be related to activation strength?

Advanced Questions

1. How could you use what you know about priming to give advice to people teaching children how to read?

2. How could the Lexical Decision task be used to test attentional processes in depressed patients?

Discsussion Questions

1. Discuss how Lexical Decision tasks support a connectionist model.

2. Discuss some potential problems that bilingual individuals might have with the storage and processing of lexical information.

Categorical Perception (Identification)

People perceive most stimuli continuously. For example, when you look at a rainbow, you see a smooth transition from red to yellow (like the image below):

You usually do not perceive stimuli categorically. Categorical perception means that you see either pure red or pure yellow and nothing in between (like the image below):

This is called "categorical" perception because instead of getting a percept that is ambiguous, you get a percept that perfectly matches an ideal example of a particular category. One thing that people seem to perceive categorically is speech (Harnard, 1987). What is interesting about this is that even when the physical stimuli change continuously (like the upper image), people perceive it categorically (like the lower image).

For example, both /b/ and /p/ are stop consonants: To produce these, you close your lips, then open them, release some air, and the vocal chords begin vibrating. Hold your hand in front of your mouth and say /ba/ and then /pa/. The difference between /ba/ and /pa/ is the time between the release of the air and the beginning of the vibration. This is referred to as voice onset time or VOT. For /b/, VOT is very short; voicing begins at almost the same time as the air is released. For /p/, the voicing is delayed.

Researchers can construct a series of stimuli in which the VOT changes in small steps. When people are asked to identify these stimuli, they generally have no difficulty: the first few are identified as /b/ and the second few are identified as /p/. What is most interesting is how the middle items are identified. Unlike most other stimuli, people do not report hearing something that is a bit like /b/ and a bit like /p/. Rather, they report hearing either /b/ or /p/.

To demonstrate categorical perception of speech stimuli, you really need two different measures. This lab provides one of those measures: it lets you find the point at which your percept changes from BA to PA through an identification task. The second (which is provided in the Categorical Perception - Discrimination experiment) examines your ability to tell whether two tokens are the same or different.

For registration information go to http://coglab.wadsworth.com.

This lab requires a computer that can play sound. Before the demonstration begins, make sure the volume on your computer/speakers is set to a comfortable level. If you are running this lab in a public space, please use headphones so that you do not disturb other people. Click once on the 'Next Trial' button to hear a sound. Your task is to report what it most sounds like.

Click once on the 'Ba' button if you think the sound was most like 'Ba' or click once on the 'Pa' button if you think the sound was most like 'Pa'.

Occasionally, the sound that is played might be distorted. If you did not hear the sound clearly, click once on the 'Redo' button instead of on the 'Ba' or 'Pa' buttons. The trial will be repeated later on in the experiment. There are 10 trials for each stimulus, for a total of 90 trials.

At the end of the experiment, you will see how many times you labeled each stimulus as "BA". The typical result is to find that you labeled the first few items as "BA" 10 out of 10 times. You should also find that labeled the last few items as "BA" 0 out of 10 times. If you perceived the stimuli categorically, you should find that there is a quick drop in the number of times you labeled an item as "BA". The quicker the decrease (i.e., if you go from 10 out of 10 on stimulus 5 to 0 out of 10 on stimulus 6), the more categorical your perception.

Additional References

Cermak, L. S., Hill, R., & Wong, B. M. (1998). Effects of spacing and repetition on amnesic patients' performance during perceptual identification stem completion, and category exemplar production. *Neuropsychology, 12*(1), 65-77.

Postle, B. & Corkin, S. (1998). Impaired word-stem completion priming but intact perceptual identification priming with novel words: Evidence from the amnesic patient H.M. *Neuropsychologia, 36*, 421-440.

Stevenage, S. (1998). Which twin are you? A demonstration of induced categorical perception of identical twin faces. *British Journal of Psychology, 89*(1), 39-58.

Basic Questions

1. Why were the endpoints of the vocal continuum, "ba" and "pa", easier to identify than the sounds in the middle?

2. Where, in the stimuli continuum between "ba" and "pa", were more errors or misidentifications made?

3. While you are waiting to see your dentist, you notice a pretty picture in the corner of the reception area. It is hard to make out the detail from where you are sitting, but it looks like a moose in a swamp. As you walk towards it to get a better look, you suddenly stop because you now see two children playing on a beach. When you are right in front of the picture, you definitely see children on a beach. Describe what you have just experienced.

4. You are unloading groceries from the car when you hear music coming from the house. It sounds like, <u>Help me Rhonda</u> by the Beach Boys, and you start singing the chorus. When you get into the house, it doesn't sound like the Beach Boys anymore and you find out that it was really <u>Jailhouse Rock</u> by Elvis Presley. Your roommate thinks you should get your hearing tested. How can you use the results of this lab to put her mind at ease about what you thought you heard?

5. If the endpoints of two categories were "night" and "day", what is one constantly changing stimulus you could use to help you to identify whether it was night or day if you didn't have a watch?

Advanced Questions

1. What could you infer about categorical perception if a number of studies found that babies could identify categories, like mom and dad (or not mom) or their cat and dog?

2. While visiting a busy city, you have your wallet stolen. Based on your description, the police want you to look through a book of potential individuals to see if your thief was in there. You think that the people all look familiar, but you narrow it down to 3 people. How could reaction time be used to determine the reliability of your choices if the three faces took 5 seconds, 15 seconds and 25 seconds to identify as the potential thief?

3. You have signed up to do a research project on perceptual identification using faces as stimuli. At one end is a typical female face and at the other end is a typical male face and there are slight facial morphs in between. What could the researcher use as dependent measures? What would each measure tell us about this psychological phenomenon?

Discussion Questions

1. This lab explored the identification of sounds and the errors that we make. Do you think trained individuals, like a musician or conductor, would make fewer errors or would they be able to identify changes in sounds, tones or pitch more quickly than the non-trained person? Explain your answer.

2. Explain how top-down (experience to physical stimuli) and bottom-up (physical stimuli to psychological experience) can influence our perceptual abilities? Examples may help to support your answer.

Categorical Perception (Discrimination)

People perceive most stimuli continuously. For example, when you look at a rainbow, you see a smooth transition from red to yellow (like the image below):

You usually do not perceive stimuli categorically. Categorical perception means that you see either pure red or pure yellow, and nothing in between (like the image below):

This is called "categorical" perception because instead of getting a percept that is ambiguous, you get a percept that perfectly matches an ideal example of a particular category. One thing that people seem to perceive categorically is speech (Harnard, 1987). What is interesting about this is that even when the physical stimuli change continuously (like the upper image), people perceive it categorically (like the lower image).

For example, both /b/ and /p/ are stop consonants: To produce these, you close your lips, then open them, release some air, and the vocal chords begin vibrating. Hold your hand in front of your mouth and say /ba/ and then /pa/. The difference between /ba/ and /pa/ is the time between the release of the air and the beginning of the vibration. This is referred to as voice onset time or VOT. For /b/, VOT is very short; voicing begins at almost the same time as the air is released. For /p/, the voicing is delayed.

Researchers can construct a series of stimuli in which the VOT changes in small steps. When people are asked to identify these stimuli, they generally have no difficulty: the first few are identified as /b/ and the second few are identified as /p/. What is most interesting is how the middle items are identified. Unlike most other stimuli, people do not report hearing something that is a bit like /b/ and a bit like /p/. Rather, they report hearing either /b/ or /p/.

To demonstrate categorical perception of speech stimuli, you really need two different measures. The first examines your ability to identify which sound you are hearing (and is provided in the Categorical Perception - Identification experiment). The second examines your ability to tell whether two tokens are the same or different. If you perceive the stimuli categorically, then it should be easy for you to correctly say that the tokens are different if they come from opposite sides of the category boundary. It should be very difficult for you to decide they are different if they come from the same side of the category boundary. In this lab, you will hear two sounds, and your task is to say whether they are the same or different.

For registration information go to http://coglab.wadsworth.com.

This lab requires a computer that can play sound. Before the demonstration begins, make sure the volume on your computer/speakers is set to a comfortable level. If you are running this lab in a public space, please use headphones so that you do not disturb other people.

Click once on the Next Trial button to hear two sounds. Your task is to report whether they are the same or different. If you think they are the same, click once on the 'Same' button. If you think they are different, click once on the 'Different' button.

Occasionally, a sound might be distorted. If you did not hear the sound clearly, click once on the 'Redo' button instead of the 'Same or 'Different' buttons. The trial will be repeated later on in the experiment. There are 140 trials.

At the end of the experiment, you will see a list of pairs of stimuli and how many times you labeled the pair as "Same". The typical result is to find that you labeled any comparisons between stimuli 1, 2, 3, and 4 as Same, and any comparisons between stimuli 6, 7, 8, and 9 as Same. This is because these stimuli all come from the same side of the category boundary. For comparisons that include stimuli from opposite sides of the boundary (especially comparisons between stimuli 4 and 6), you should find these labeled "Different".

Additional References

Levin, D. (2000). Race as a visual feature: Using visual search and perceptual discrimination tasks to understand face categories and the cross-race recognition deficit. *Journal of Experimental Psychology: General, 129*, 559-574.

Stark, C. & Squire, L. (2000). Intact visual perceptual discrimination in humans in the absence of perirhinal cortex. *Learning and Memory, 7*(5), 273-278.

Basic Questions

1. What is the difference between "ba" and "pa" in terms of the voice onset time (VOT) that helps us to discriminate between these sounds?

2. According to the CogLab introduction, should stimuli 4 and 6 be determined as the same or different? Why or why not?

3. After reading through the literature, you discover that light blue is a calming color. You are having trouble sleeping, so you decide to paint your bedroom walls light blue. The salesclerk at the hardware store only has dark blue, but reassures you that she can make light blue by adding white paint to it. The clerk adds some white paint, but you still think it is a dark blue. She continues to add white paint, but you still think it looks like the same paint color she started with. The clerk adds the last bit of white paint she has and this time you think it is the light blue that you wanted. How could that small bit of white paint make a difference between dark and light blue paint?

4. Discuss the general problems that a color-blind person has in discriminating between colors?

5. Your dentist is trying to determine the extent of damage you have in your wisdom tooth to see if it is worth saving or if he should pull it out. He pokes at your tooth in a sensitive spot and you jump in pain. On a scale from 1-10, you rate the pain as a 7. He continues to poke your tooth in different places and asks you each time if that was more painful or about the same amount of pain as the last poke. Explain how he is using categorical discrimination to determine the extent of the damage to your tooth?

Advanced Questions

1. Do you think it would be easier to discriminate between 5 and 10 pound weights or between 70 and 75 pound weights? Explain your answer.

2. What discrimination task would your optometrist use if she were trying to determine if your eyesight had changed from –4.5 to –5.0?

3. You are trying to make juice, but you are not sure how much sugar should be used (you have determined that the packages always tell you to put in more sugar than necessary). You decide to try adding a small amount of sugar and then tasting it to see if it is enough. You start off with 1/3 cup, but that is not enough; then another 1/3 cup, but you still can't taste a difference. After adding another 1/3 cup, you find it too sweet. Instead of adding another 1/3 cup the third time, what amount should you have added, knowing what you know about the boundary between sweet and sour?

Discussion Questions

1. Signal detection theory can be used to help explain the errors that we make in categorical perception. Discuss the four scenarios of signal detection (hit, miss, false alarm and correct rejection) in relation to the errors and reaction time in discriminating between "ba" and "pa".

2. We have to socially discriminate between different categories of people, for example between honest/dishonest or funny/not funny. Although these characteristics follow a continuum, we don't usually describe someone as kind of honest or a bit funny? Give a specific example of a continuous behavior that we subjectively label as one way or another and discuss how we may be able to discriminate between the two categories. Don't use the examples already given. Indicate if setting the parameters between the 2 categories of behaviors is easy or hard to do and why.

224

11.1 GESTALT APPROACH TO PROBLEM SOLVING

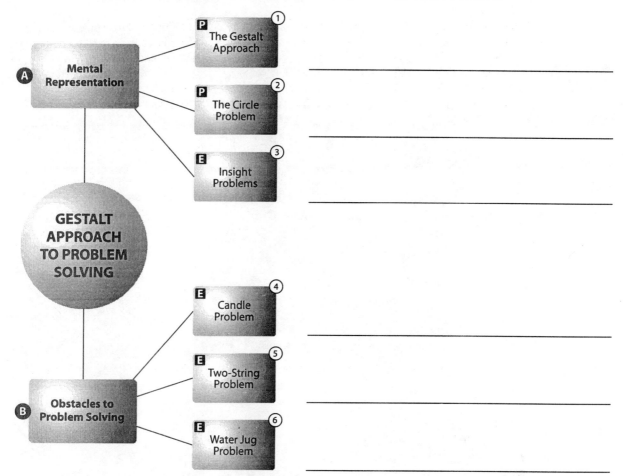

A How did the Gestalt psychologists approach the study of problem solving?

① **Principle:** What two processes are involved in problem solving, according to the Gestalt psychologists? (390)

② **Principle:** How does the circle problem demonstrate the ideas of representation and restructuring in problem solving? (390)

③ **Experiment:** Describe the experiment that compared how participants progressed toward a solution for insight problems and non-insight problems. (Metcalfe & Wiebe; 391)

B How did the Gestalt psychologists demonstrate different obstacles to problem solving?

④ **Experiment:** Describe the candle problem and the results of the experiments that asked participants to solve this problem. How do the results of these experiments demonstrate an effect called functional fixedness? (Duncker; Adamson; 392)

⑤ **Experiment:** Describe the experiment that investigated the two-string problem. How does the result illustrate functional fixedness? (Maier; 395)

⑥ **Experiment:** Describe the water jug problem. How does the result illustrate mental set? (Luchins; 396)

11.2 SEARCH AND ANALOGY

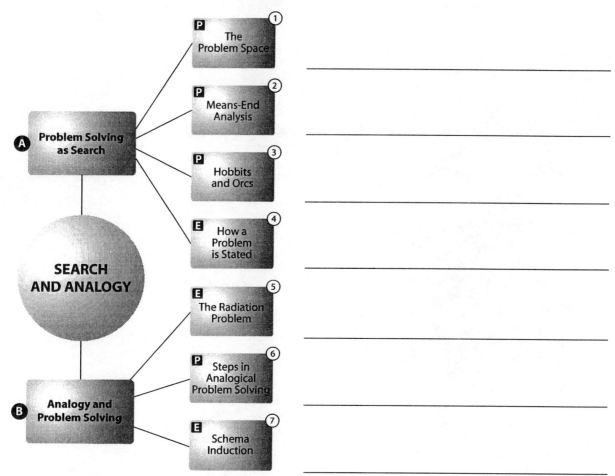

A How can problem solving be seen as a process of searching?

① **Principle:** What is the problem space, and how can problem solving be described as occurring within the problem space? (398)

② **Principle:** What is means-end analysis, and how can it be illustrated by (a) solving the Tower of Hanoi problem; and (b) solving an "everyday" problem? (399)

③ **Principle:** What does the solution to the Hobbits and Orcs problem illustrate about means-end analysis? (401)

④ **Experiment:** Describe the mutilated checkerboard problem. How was it used to show that people's ability to solve a problem can depend on the way the problem is presented? (Kaplan & Simon; 402) What do this problem and the Monk and the mountain problem illustrate about using analogies to solve problems? (405)

B How can analogies be used to facilitate problem solving?

⑤ **Experiment:** What is Dunker's radiation problem? Describe the experiment that used "The General" story to find a solution to the radiation problem. (Gick & Holyoak; 408)

⑥ **Principle:** What are the three steps that are involved in analogical problem solving? Which one is the most difficult to achieve? (410)

⑦ **Experiment:** Describe the schema induction experiment that involved the "Fire Chief" story. What is the relationship between goodness of schemas and the ability to solve the radiation problem? (Gick & Holyoak; 412)

11.3 EXPERTISE AND CREATIVITY

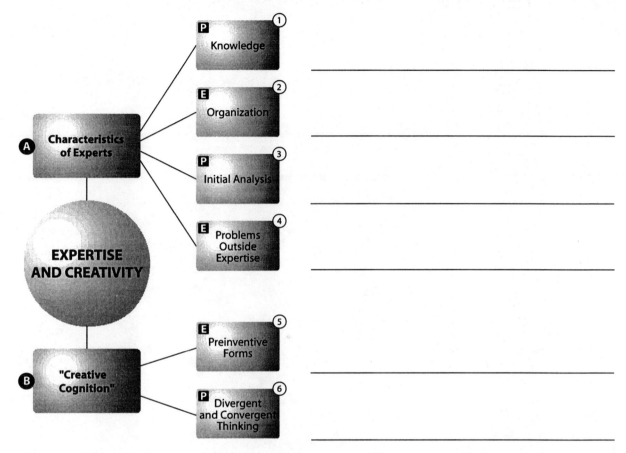

A How do experts and non-experts solve problems?

① **Principle:** How did knowledge help expert chess players outperform novices in reproducing positions on a chess board? (414)

② **Experiment:** Describe the experiment that compared the way experts and novices go about solving physics problems. (Chi; 414)

③ **Principle:** Why do experts often get off to a slow start in solving problems? (415)

④ **Experiment:** How well do experts perform when solving problems in a field outside their area of expertise? (Voss; 416)

B What is "creative cognition"?

⑤ **Experiment:** Describe the experiment in which people were given a task that involved creating preinventive forms. (Finke; 417)

⑥ **Principle:** Compare divergent and convergent thinking. (420)

12.1 DEDUCTIVE REASONING I

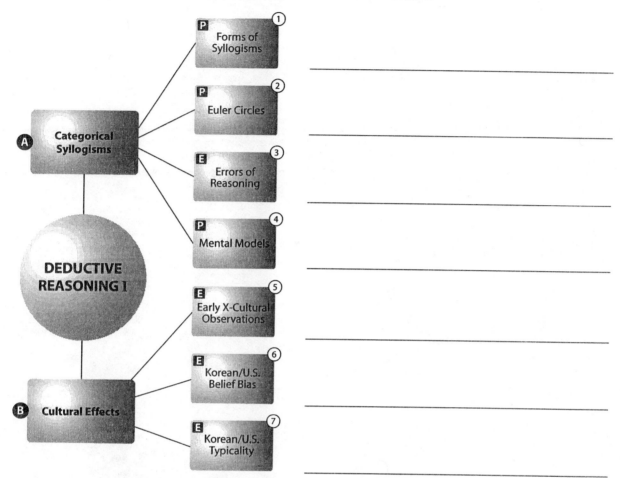

A **What are the properties of categorical syllogisms?**

① **Principle:** What is the basic form of a categorical syllogism? Which forms are valid and which are not valid? What are the first two principles of deductive reasoning? (430)

② **Principle:** How can the validity of syllogisms be determined using Euler circles? What is the third principle of deductive reasoning? (432)

③ **Experiment:** What is the atmosphere effect? The belief bias? Describe the results of the experiment in which people were asked to judge the validity of syllogisms with believable and non-believable conclusions. (Evans; 436)

④ **Principle:** Describe the mental model approach to determining the validity of syllogisms. What requirement of mental model theory must be fulfilled to determine whether or not a syllogism is valid? (437)

B **How is deductive reasoning affected by culture?**

⑤ **Experiment:** Describe the cross-cultural experiments that were carried out by Sylvia Scribner. What did she conclude about the kind of evidence her participants used to answer her questions about syllogisms? (Scribner; 440)

⑥ **Experiment:** Describe the experiment that compared the belief bias in European-Americans and Korean participants. (Norenzayan; 441)

⑦ **Experiment:** Describe the experiment that compared how European-Americans, Asian-Americans, and Koreans performed on a task in which they evaluated statements that referred to typical and non-typical members of a category. (Norenzayan; 441)

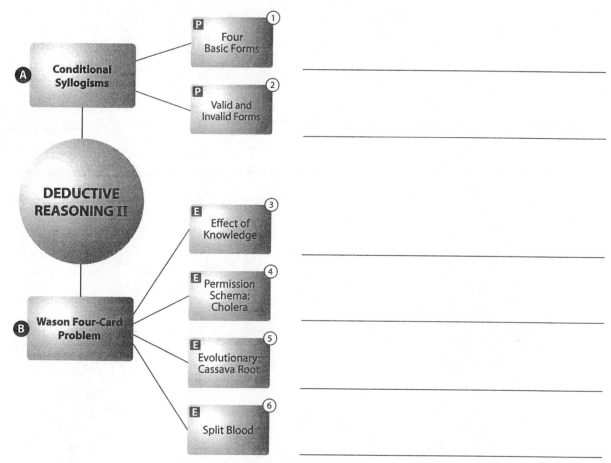

A   **What are the properties of conditional syllogisms?**

①   **Principle:** What are the four basic forms of conditional syllogisms? (443)

②   **Principle:** Which two forms of conditional syllogisms are valid and which two forms are not valid? (444)

B   **What does the Wason four-card problem tell us about conditional reasoning?**

③   **Experiments:** Compare performance on the Wason four-card problem for (a) the original abstract version (Wason); (b) the beer/drinking age version (Griggs and Cox); and (c) the postal regulation version (Johnson-Laird; Griggs & Cox). What do all of these experiments, taken together, suggest about the role of knowledge in solving the problem? (446)

④   **Experiment:** Describe the "cholera" experiment. Indicate how the results support the idea that better performance on "real world" versions of the Wason task can be explained in terms of pragmatic reasoning schemas. (Cheng & Holyoak; 450)

⑤   **Experiment:** What is the evolutionary perspective on cognition, and how has social exchange theory been applied to the Wason task? Describe the "cassava root" experiment that tested the idea of social exchange. (Cosmides & Tooby; 451)

⑥   **Experiment:** Describe the "spilt blood" experiment that was designed in response to the social exchange proposal. (Mantelow & Over; 452) Has the controversy involving different explanations of the Wason task been resolved?

12.3 INDUCTIVE REASONING I

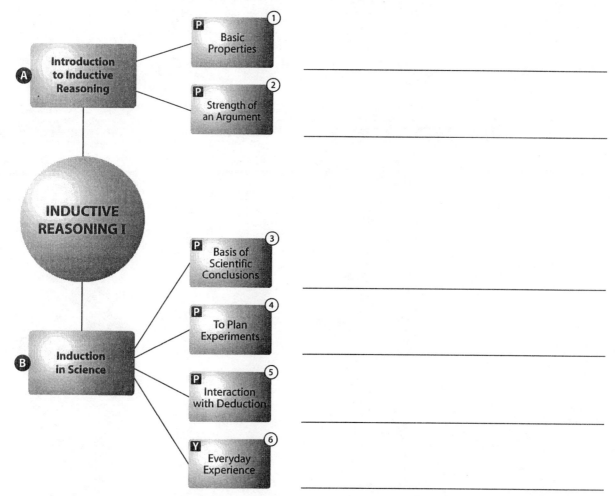

A **What are the properties of inductive reasoning?**

① **Principle:** What is the form of inductive arguments, and how does inductive reasoning differ from deductive reasoning? (454)

② **Principle:** What are three factors that contribute to the strength of an inductive argument? (455)

B **How is inductive reasoning used in science?**

③ **Principle:** What does it mean to say that inductive reasoning is the basic procedure used to make scientific discoveries? (456)

④ **Principle:** Give an example of how inductive reasoning is used to plan experiments. (456)

⑤ **Principle:** What is the connection between inductive and deductive reasoning in scientific research? (456)

⑥ **Your Experience:** Think of a few examples of how you have used inductive reasoning to make choices in your life.

12.4 INDUCTIVE REASONING II

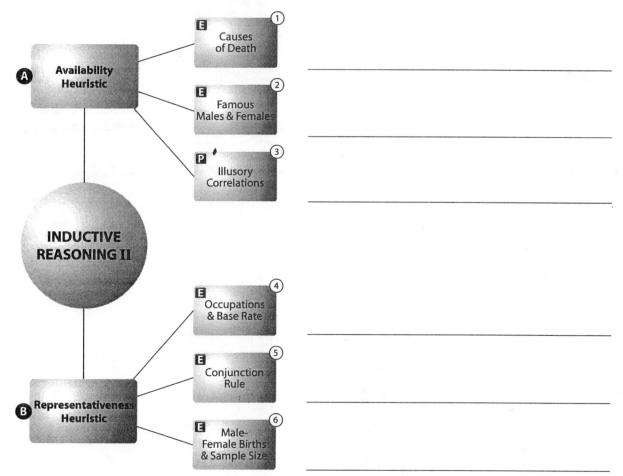

(A) **What is the availability heuristic, and how does it influence our choices?**

(1) **Experiment:** What were the results of the experiment in which participants were asked to judge the relative prevalence of various causes of death? How can these results be explained by the availability heuristic? (Lichtenstein; 458)

(2) **Experiment:** Describe the "famous men/famous women" experiment and how the results may have been influenced by the availability heuristic. (McKelvie; 460)

(3) **Principle:** What are illusory correlations and how are they related to stereotyping? (460)

(B) **What is the representativeness heuristic, and how does it influence our judgments?**

(4) **Experiment:** Describe the experiment in which people were asked to guess a person's occupation. How is the result related to the representativeness heuristic and to ignoring base rate information? (Kahneman & Tversky; 461)

(5) **Experiment:** What is the conjunction rule? What happened when people ignored it when they were asked to decide if Linda was a bank teller or a feminist bank teller? (Tversky & Kahneman; 462)

(6) **Experiment:** Describe the experiment in which people were asked to decide which hospitals would have more days when there were more male than female births. How does the result of this experiment relate to the law of large numbers? (Tversky & Kahneman; 463)

12.5 INDUCTIVE REASONING III

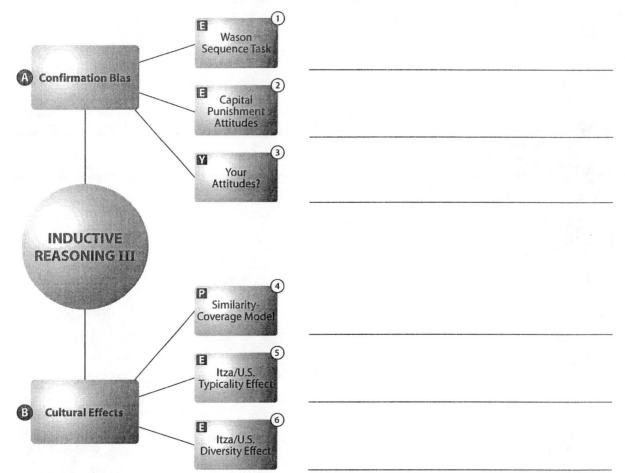

A **What is the confirmation bias, and how does it affect our judgments?**

① **Experiment:** Describe the Wason selection task. How can the results of Wason's experiment be related to the confirmation bias? (Wason; 464)

② **Experiment:** Describe the experiment that investigated how peoples' attitudes about capital punishment are influenced by contradictory evidence. How is the result related to the confirmation bias? (Lord; 465)

③ **Your Experience:** Can you think of a situation in which you paid more attention to evidence that supported your attitudes or beliefs and less attention to evidence that contradicted your attitudes or beliefs?

B **How is inductive reasoning affected by culture?**

④ **Principle:** Describe the similarity-coverage model and the principles of typicality and diversity that follow from this model. (466)

⑤ **Experiment:** Describe the experiment in which Itza and U.S. participants were presented with inductive arguments that led to the conclusion "all mammals have an ulnar artery". How did the two groups respond with regard to the principle of typicality? (Lopez; 467)

⑥ **Experiment:** For the experiment above, how did the two groups respond with regard to the principle of diversity? What is the explanation for the result? (Lopez; 467)

12.6 DECISION MAKING

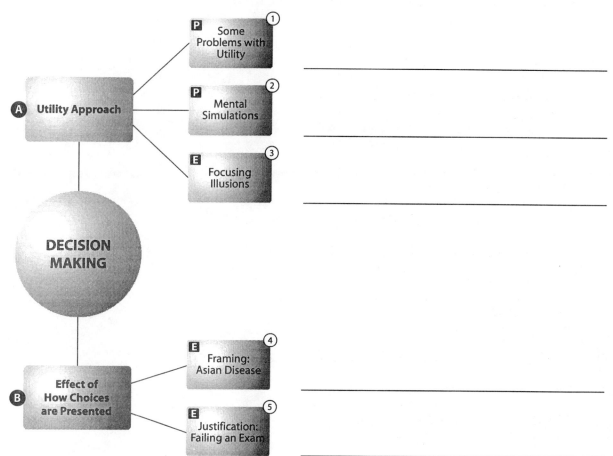

A **What is the utility approach to decision making, and how well does it describe peoples' behavior?**

① **Principle:** Describe two problems with the utility approach that can be illustrated by (a) people's gambling behavior; and (b) the ability to calculate payoffs. (469)

② **Principle:** What is a mental simulation? How can the use of mental simulations pose problems for the utility approach to decisions? (469)

③ **Experiment:** What is the focusing illusion? How was it demonstrated in an experiment that concerned peoples' perceptions about the desirability of living in California or the Midwest? (Wilson; 470)

B **How does the way in which choices are presented affect peoples' decisions?**

④ **Experiment:** Describe the "Asian disease" experiment. How is the framing effect illustrated by the results of this experiment? Under what conditions do people adopt risk-averse and risk-taking strategies? (Tversky & Kahneman; 471)

⑤ **Experiment:** Describe the experiment in which people read a story about failing or passing an exam, and were then asked to decide whether they would buy a vacation package. How can the result be explained in terms of "justification"? (Tversky & Shafir; 473)

Wason Selection Task

Research has shown that people find it very difficult to decide what information is necessary in order to test the truth of an abstract logical reasoning problem. The Wason Selection Task is often used to examine this issue.

A typical experiment using the Wason Selection Task will present some rule, and ask subjects to see if the rule is being violated. Consider the rule: If a card has a D on one side, it has a 3 on the other side. Subjects are aware that on the particular set of cards, each one has a letter on one side and a number on the other side. Four cards are shown, such as those below:

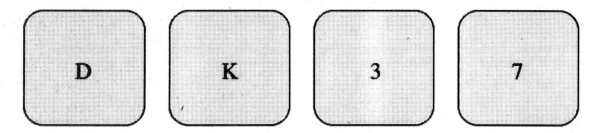

Very few people can correctly pick the two cards to turn over to verify the rule. The correct cards are D and 7; most likely, you picked D and 3. Seeing what is on the reverse of the 7 card can lead to falsifying the rule if a D shows up. Seeing what is on the reverse of the 3 card cannot falsify the rule. It can confirm the rule, but not falsify it.

Consider another rule: If you borrow my car, you must fill up the gas tank. Four cards are shown below:

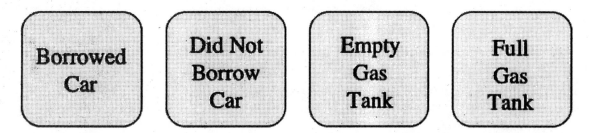

Which cards do you turn over to see if the rule is being followed? You should find that now the answer is more obvious: You want to know what's on the reverse of "borrowed car" and "empty gas tank".

This lab is based on a series of experiments reported by Wason & Shapiro (1971). You will be given a series of rules to verify. Half of them are abstract and half are thematic (the same kind of rule shown

243

above about borrowing a car). The basic idea is that you can test rules when you have some knowledge or experience that is appropriate, but not when you lack this experience. In the thematic case, then, you are not really using logic per se but rather your experience. In the abstract case, you cannot use your experience and have to rely solely on logic.

For registration information go to http://coglab.wadsworth.com.

Start a trial by clicking on the Next Trial button. You will see a rule and four buttons. The rule will ask about two kinds of events. Your task is to select two cards to see what is on the other side so that you can see if the rule is true or false. To select a card, simply click on the appropriate button. Once you have clicked on a card, you cannot change your response.

There are 6 trials, 3 with abstract and 3 with thematic rules.

When the experiment finishes, a new window will appear that gives the proportion of correct solutions for both the abstract and the thematic rules. You should find that you did very well on the thematic rules, but quite poorly on the abstract rules. In the thematic case, your knowledge helps you arrive at a correct solution, whereas you have no knowledge to help in the thematic case.

Additional References

Almor A. & Sloman, S. A. (2000). Reasoning versus memory in the Wason selection task - A non-deontic perspective on perspective effects. *Memory and Cognition, 28*, 1060-1069.

Cosmides, L. (1989). The logic of social exchange: Has natural selection shaped how humans reason? Studies with the Wason selection task. *Cognition, 31,* 187-276.

Platt, R. D., & Griggs, R. A. (1993). Darwinian algorithms and the Wason selection task: A factorial analysis of social contract selection task problems. *Cognition, 48*, 163-192.

Yachanin, S.A. (1986). Facilitation in Wason's selection task: Content and instructions. *Current Psychological Research and Review, (5)* 20-29.

Basic Questions

1. When the conditional rule is stated this way, "if p, then q", this is a(n) _____ (abstract or concrete) statement, whereas "if you get bit by a poisonous snake, you will die is an example of a(n) _____ statement.

2. Of the two types of conditional rules, abstract or concrete, which is usually easier for people to solve?

3. You tell your brother in the morning after he eats his breakfast, "If you leave the milk out of the refrigerator, it will go bad". Could you assume that your brother left the milk out if you tasted the milk that evening and it was sour? Why or why not?

4. Your biggest pet peeve is liars; you can't stand it when people lie to you. You think your friend lied to you but you are not sure. You tell him that if you catch him lying to you, you will never speak to him again. Your friend wants to test your rule, so he lies to you, but you do not stop speaking to him. Can your friend say that your rule was not correct? If you stopped speaking to him one week later, what would have to be true to make this a logically correct rule?

Advanced Questions

1. You are a division manager for a large corporation that makes toothpicks. You have noticed that your division is spending a lot in wages, but your toothpick productivity is decreasing. You want to fire those individuals who are on the payroll, but are not packaging at least 100 boxes of toothpicks per day. Give an example of the conditional rule you could send out to the members of your division so that if they did not follow the rule, they could be fired.

2. Your mother made a couple of batches of cookies, and they are cooling in the kitchen. As she is leaving the kitchen she tells that you can have some cookies, but says that you can't eat the batch of cookies on the green plate because she mixed up the ingredients and put rat poison in them and you will get sick if you eat them; however, she says it is safe to eat the cookies on the yellow plate. Your get distracted by the phone before you get to the cookies. When you get off the phone, you look at the plates while trying to remember which plate of cookies to eat from. If you had to put this example on cards (like in the lab), what would the four conditions be? Which conditional rule would you not want to test?

3. You are doing some volunteer work in the hospital one summer when you run into a big problem. The nurse on duty tells you that if you do not give Mr. Jones his medication at 4:00 pm, he will not be very cooperative for the night nurse. The following day, you read the note from the night nurse who is not happy with you because Mr. Jones was not very cooperative. What are the two possible assumptions that the night nurse could have about Mr. Jones' medication on the previous day? Which assumption would make this rule logically correct? Which assumption is logically incorrect to make?

Discussion Questions

1. Discuss some further examples of conditional rules that society places on us every day so we can function properly as a group, instead of as selfish individuals. These can be legal, moral, psychological, etc. rules.

2. Discuss why some researchers feel the Wason Selection Task may be related to memory processes and not deductive reasoning. Did you find that you were remembering a rule that helped you with the examples in the lab, or were you analyzing the logic of the rules?

Typical Reasoning

Tversky and Kahneman (1983) are well known for their research showing that people's estimates of probability are often very different from the objective probabilities. The reason, they argue, is that people often use heuristics to help them estimate the answer. Heuristics can be seen as sacrificing some accuracy for an increase in speed. By using heuristics, people can come up with an answer very quickly that is usually good enough for day to day purposes. These heuristics, however, can lead to incorrect judgments.

One of the most striking errors is known as the conjunction fallacy. In its most simple form, it says that people think that having both A and B occur is more likely than having just A occur or just B occur. According to objective probabilities, the probability of two events occurring has to be less than the probabilities of either of the events happening by themselves. In some circumstances, however, people are more likely to say the conjunction (having both events occur) is more likely.

In particular, the conjunction fallacy is more likely when the items are typical than atypical. For example, read the following:

> Julie is 26 years old, has a degree in physical education, has been physically fit since childhood, and loves the outdoors.

People think it is more likely that Julie is a ski instructor who also teaches aerobics (a conjunction involving an activity thought to more typical of ski instructors) than that Julie is a librarian who also teaches aerobics (a conjunction involving an activity thought to be less typical of librarians). When the activity is particularly typical, then the conjunction can be thought more likely than the single events (e.g., that Julie is a ski instructor).

This demonstration is based on an experiment by Shafir, Smith, and Osherson (1990). You will read short descriptions about several people, and you will be asked to rate the probability that these people have certain professions and/or engage in certain activities.

For registration information go to http://coglab.wadsworth.com.

Start a trial by clicking once on the 'Next Trial' button. After clicking on the experiment, a window will appear. Start a trial by clicking once on the "Next Trial" button. You will be shown a short description of a person. Read the description carefully. After each description, you will be asked to judge how likely it is, on a scale from 0 to 7, that the person has a particular profession or engages in a particular activity. For example, you might be asked the following:

> How likely is it that Bob bets on horse racing?

If you are absolutely certain, based on the description of him that you have just read, that Bob would never bet on horse racing, click on the "0 = Impossible" button. If you are absolutely certain that Bob bets on horse racing, click on the "7 = Certain" button.

246

There are no correct or incorrect answers. Please respond based on the assumption that the person described is a real person. There are only 12 trials, so please read each description carefully before responding.

When the experiment finishes, a new window will appear that reports your mean ratings for each of four types of judgments. There are four types of statements associated with each person's description, but you saw only one. The four statements include one with an event that is not typical given the person's description; one with an event that is very typical; one statement with the atypical event combined with a profession; and one statement with the typical event combined with a profession.

You should find that for the single events, you gave higher ratings for the typical event than for the atypical event. For the conjunctions, you should find that you gave higher ratings for the typical than for the atypical conjunction. You should also find that you have rated conjunctions with typical activities as more likely than single typical events. If you were relying on objective probabilities, the conjunctions should have been rated as less likely than the single events.

Additional References

Fantino, E., Kulik, J., Stolarz-Fantino, S., & Wright, W. (1997). The conjunction fallacy: A test of averaging hypotheses. *Psychonomic Bulletin & Review, 4*, 96-101.

Fisk, J. & Pidgeon, N. (1997). The conjunction fallacy: The case for the existence of competing heuristic strategies. *British Journal of Psychology, 88*, 1-27.

Basic Questions

1. Bob is 32 and is very athletic. When he is not playing sports, he has his head buried in a book about health and fitness.
    - Give an example of each of the four scenarios used in this lab (single typical, single atypical, conjunctive atypical, conjunctive atypical)?

2. Why would your chances of finding a good used car decrease if your requirements are that it has to be red, a 4-door, good on gas, and under $1000?

3. You are writing a paper on gambling for Health Psychology. You are frustrated because the Internet search is not helping you to find any scientific journals on the effects of gambling on your immune system, but you know they exist. You are using some the keywords, "gambling" and "health" and "immune system". How could you change your search strategy so you could increase the number of hits you get?

4. One of your duties as the recreation director for a summer sport's camp is to find quality camp counselors. You are really busy with final exams and don't have a great deal of time to interview a lot of people. How could you reduce the number of applications that you receive without cutting the quality of the applicants?

5. Saturday afternoon you go to the local library to do some research for a paper. You are having trouble finding a journal so you look for the librarian. You notice 2 people who look like they are working, one is a female about 45 and is wearing glasses and the other is a female about 25 without glasses. You immediately approach the older female who refers you to the other woman as the librarian. Why did you quickly assume the older woman was the librarian?

Advanced Questions

1. Police profilers are portrayed on television as being able to determine, with accuracy, the probability that an individual has committed a crime based on a combination of personality traits and situational circumstances. Why does this seem like an inaccurate way of determining guilt given what you have learned from this lab?

2. Some people with specific occupations rely on making life and death decisions quickly. When accuracy is more important than speed, what type of reasoning should individuals adopt and why? (Think of the 4 scenarios discussed in this lab.)

3. You are a doorman in a popular nightclub. Lately there have been a number of fights in the club and your boss wants you to stop them before they start. While scanning the crowd for potential fights, 2 large groups of individuals come in. You can't watch both groups simultaneously, so you have to decide which group to focus more attention on. One group is made up of longhaired males, while the other group is also made up of some longhaired males and some men with shaved heads with noticeable tattoos. Which group do you think is more likely to start a fight and why? Have you made any errors calculating probability?

Discussion Questions

1. Results from this lab help demonstrate that sometimes we perceive something to be more probable than it really is, resulting in estimation errors. How does this help to explain phobias that people may develop, like fear of flying or the fear of the number 13 (Triskadekaphobia)?

2. What would you suggest a university could do to reduce the number of errors made from stereotyping people or groups of people based on characteristics they portray?

Risky Decisions

Our lives are full of decisions. We must choose what books to read, movies to see, courses to take, person to date, routes to drive, and thousands of other decisions every day. You might hope that people weigh their options carefully and make the best decision possible. Studies in cognitive psychology, however, tell us that the way people make decisions is influenced by a variety of factors. In fact, it is fairly easy to create contexts where people choose certain options. Many of these tendencies are called "framing effects," because the perceived context or way the choices are "framed" make a big difference, even for situations that are otherwise equivalent. Framing effects have been noted for centuries, and many were summarized by Kahneman and Tversky (1982).

To understand some of these framing effects, we need to distinguish between two types of decision making choices: risky and riskless. A risky choice is one where there is a probability or chance of different possibilities occurring. For example, if you decide to spend money on a lottery, there is an unknown outcome. You may win a lot of money, or you may not. The final outcome is not made by your decision; your decision simply enters you into a probabilistic situation. A riskless choice is one where the ultimate outcome is decided by the choice. For example, if you decide to invest your money in a bank account and earn interest, you have made a riskless choice.

Different people are comfortable with different amounts of risk. Some people tend to be risk-seeking and look for situations where the ultimate outcome is unknown. Other people tend to be risk-avoiding and look for the "sure bets." Regardless of your comfort level with risk, your tendency to be risk-avoiding or risk-seeking can be influenced by the context within which the options are presented to you. A common finding in the experimental literature on decision making is that people tend to be risk-seeking when the options available to them seem to involve losses. People tend to be risk-avoiding when the options available to them seem to involve gains. Interestingly, as long as you are honest in your responses, this effect does not disappear even when you know of its influence on you.

This demonstration shows how the framing of the options to look as gains or losses changes your willingness to deal with risk. Decision making experiments tend to be done by asking participants to imagine themselves in a particular situation and then to choose between two or more possibilities. This approach depends on the honesty of the participants. You can easily get invalid results by refusing to answer honestly.

This demonstration also shows another common finding in studies of decision making: changes tend to be more important than final states. All of the questions in the experiment involve sums of money (U.S. dollars). There are pairs of questions that are equivalent in the sense that you will reach the same absolute amount of money, or possible amount of money in a risky option, for either question in a pair. If your decision making was based solely on the final amount of money you would have, you would make the same decision for either member of the pair. Odds are, however, that you will behave quite differently across the pair members; choosing the risky option for one question but the riskless option for the other. Many aspects of economics and business pertain to properties of decision making. The old business adage of focusing on the "bottom line" is an effort to avoid the tendency among people to focus on changes instead of absolute effects. Characteristics of decision-making tendencies are also well known by advertisers and politicians, who will sometimes influence people's decisions by framing options in a certain way. You can also learn to make better decisions (in the sense of making decisions that are more in line with your beliefs) by taking a more objective approach in your daily life, and by learning some details about statistical reasoning.

For registration information go to http://coglab.wadsworth.com.

After clicking on the start button, a window will appear. Start a trial by pressing the space bar. You will be asked to imagine that you have (above and beyond what you currently own) an extra amount of money. This amount will vary across questions. You will see two options and you will be asked which one you would prefer. For example, you might see:

Imagine you have been given $350

Which would you choose?

A: A sure loss of $60

OR

B: 0.4 probability of losing $0 and 0.6 probability of losing $100

If you pick Option A, you will have a final total of $290 because you are guaranteed to lose $60. If you pick Option B, you might lose nothing (and keep all $350) but you might lose $100 and end up with only $250. For this example, if you picked Option B, you would lose $100 six times out of ten.

To indicate your preference, type the letter that corresponds to the option that you think is best. If you prefer Option A, press the a key. If you prefer Option B, press the b key. You may change your choice before starting the next trial. In making your decision, try to imagine what the money would actually be worth to you. For example, if you owe a threatening loan shark $290, perhaps it is better to pick the riskless situation (option A) so that you are certain to be able to completely pay off the debt. On the other hand, if you really need $350, and having $290 will not suffice, perhaps it is better to take the risky option (option B) and hope you keep all the money. You should make the decision relative to your real world situation (which is hopefully not so stressful). Some people will like option A best and some will like option B best; there are no absolutely correct answers.

Other trials include options with gains instead of losses of money. The starting amount of money, the loss or gain amounts, and the probabilities vary across trials. After you are satisfied with your choice, press the space bar to start the next trial. There are a total of 30 trials.

When the experiment finishes, a new window will appear that reports the percentage of times you selected the risky option (option B), for the gain questions and the loss questions. The expected result is that the percentage will be higher for the questions where the options available are both losses of money than for the questions where the options available are both gains of money.

Additional References

Fagley, N. S., & Miller, P. M. (1990). The effect of framing on choice: Interactions with risk-taking propensity, cognitive style, and sex. *Personality and Social Psychology Bulletin, 16*, 496-510.

Kuhberger, A. (1998). The influence of framing on risky decisions: A meta-analysis. *Organizational Behavior and Human Decision Processes, 75*, 23-55.

Mayhorn, C. B., Fisk, A. D. & Whittle, J. D. (2002). Decisions, decisions: analysis of age, cohort, and time of testing on framing of risky decision options. *Human Factors, 44*(4), 515-522.
Wiseman, D. B. & Levin, L. P. (1996). Comparing risky decision making under conditions of real and hypothetical consequences. *Organizational Behavior and Human Decision Processes, 66*, 241-250.

Basic Questions

1. How would you know if your results supported a framing effect?

2. Give an example (not presented here) of a risky decision and a riskless decision

3. When do people generally seek a risky decision?

4. What are the expected results for this CogLab?

5. If a person was a risk-avoiding person, do you think they would buy a lottery ticket where there was a 1 in 5 chance of winning, but the prize was very small, or would they buy a ticket with a grand prize with a 1/5000 of winning?

Advanced Questions

1. How could companies use framing effects in their commercials?

2. How might the leader of a country be influenced by framing effect?

Discussion Questions

1. Discuss the suggestion that is made in the CogLab that changes tend to be more important than final states.

2. Discuss how framing effects influence risk-taking behaviors.

Monty Hall

Most people have a poor understanding of probability. One common problem occurs when evaluating combinations of events. The Monty Hall 3 Door problem is a classic example. Based on an old TV game show, Let's Make A Deal, the problem involves 3 doors. Behind one of the doors is a prize. The contestant picks one door. Monty Hall, the eminent emcee, picks one of the remaining two doors to open and shows that the prize is not there. The question is: Do you stay with your original pick or do you change your pick? (We assume Monty Hall is playing fair and always does this.)

You originally begin with a 1 in 3 chance (0.333 probability) of picking the correct door. Many people think that it doesn't matter whether you stay with your original pick or switch after Monty reveals his door.

This interpretation is incorrect. You are better off always switching; over the long term, you will average 66% correct. If you always stay, you will average 33% correct over the long term. If you randomly switch or stay, you will average 50% over the long term.

Here's how to think of it. You begin with a 1 out of 3 chance of picking the correct door. Monty Hall shows that one of the other doors is incorrect. If you do nothing, you still have a 1/3 chance of being correct. Because you know the prize is not behind the door he opened, it must be behind the remaining door 2/3 of the time and behind the door you picked 1/3 of the time.

For registration information go to http://coglab.wadsworth.com.

This lab simulates the Monty Hall 3 Door Problem. It lets you try out the various options and see how often you would win. Start a trial by clicking on the Next Trial button. Then, select a door. One of the doors will have its contents changed from '?' to '-' to indicate there is no prize. Now, you decide whether to pick your original door again, or whether to switch. Once you either confirm your original choice or pick a new door, the winning door will be shown (with a '+') the other losing door will be shown (with a '-').

To maximize the number of wins, make your first selection randomly, and then always change to the other door. To minimize the number of wins, make your first selection randomly, then always stick with your first choice.

When the experiment finishes, a new window will appear that shows you how many times you successfully picked the winning door. If you randomly picked a door, and then randomly switched or stayed, you should be right 50% of the time. If you randomly picked a door and stayed with that choice, you should be right 33% of the time. If you randomly picked a door and always changed, you should be right 66% of the time.

Additional References

Bailey, H. (1999). Monty Hall uses a mixed strategy. *Mathematics Magazine, 73*(2), 135-141.

Baron, J. (1988). *Thinking and Deciding.* Cambridge, UK: Cambridge University Press.

Eisenhauer, J. G. (2000). The Monty Hall Matrix. *Teaching Statistics, 22*(1), 17-20.

Fernandez, L. & Piron, R. (1999). Should She Switch? A Game-Theoretic Analysis of the Monty Hall Problem. *Mathematics Magazine, 72(*3), 214-217.

Friedman, D. (1998). Monty Hall's three doors: Construction and deconstruction of a choice anomaly. *The American Economic Review, 88*, 933-946.

Kahneman, D. & Tversky, A. (1973). On the psychology of prediction. *Psychological Review, 8, 237-251*

Von Winterfeldt, D. & Edwards, W. (1986). On Cognitive Illusions and their Implications. In H. R. Arkes & K. R. Hammond (Eds.) *Judgment and decision making: An interdisciplinary reader. Cambridge, UK:* Cambridge University Press.

Basic Questions

1. Why does the probability of winning increase from a 1 in 2 chance, to a 2 in 3 chance when you always switched doors in the CogLab?

2. If a situation has 2 possible outcomes, what is the chance level or the possibility of an event occurring by chance?

3. While you were doing the lab, what would you start to think if you lost 10 times in a row? Are the losses independent or dependent of one another?

4. In the game show, "Let's Make a Deal", it was imperative that Monty Hall knew where the grand prize was so he could reveal the other losing curtain. In terms of probability, why was this imperative?

5. According to the Monty Hall principle, what should you do in the following scenario?
   "You are dating three potential females (Brenda, Stephanie and Heather) because you are looking for the perfect woman to marry. You've heard that 2/3 of all marriages end in divorce, so you want to be sure that you are that 1 couple that makes it. You decide to marry Brenda and break Stephanie and Heather's hearts. Two years later you hear that Stephanie married a friend of yours right after you broke up with her, but it recently ended in divorce. What do you do, stay with Brenda or look for Heather's phone number?

Advanced Questions

1. Your psychology professor tells the class that 1/5 of the class will fail her class because it is tough and requires a lot of work. If there are 200 people in her class, how many people will fail if her statistic is correct?

2. What would the probability of winning the grand prize be if there were 7 curtains or doors instead of 3 to begin with, but he revealed the prizes behind 2 doors?

Discussion Questions

1. Humans have problems understanding probabilities of events occurring. Discuss some of the reasons why we have these problems. For example, could these problems be due to a misunderstanding of the problem or limitations of our brains? Give examples to help support your answer.

2. The Monty Hall problem sparked a debate for a number of years among the highly intellectual academics. What do you think some of the possible reasons are for the heated debate? Discuss the problem itself and not the stubborn nature of academics.